Learning About Fall & Winter Holidays

by
Jeri A. Carroll
and
Candace B. Wells

Illustrated by Jeff Van Kanegan

Cover by Jeff Van Kanegan

Copyright © Good Apple, Inc., 1988

ISBN No. 0-86653-441-5

Printing No. 98765432

Good Apple, Inc.
Box 299
Carthage, IL 62321-0299

The purchase of this book entitles the buyer to reproduce student activity pages for classroom use only. Any other use requires written permission from Good Apple, Inc.

All rights reserved. Printed in the United States of America.

Table of Contents

Introduction iii

How to Use This Book iv

Labor Day (First Monday in September) 1

Citizenship Day (September 12) 9

Columbus Day (October 12) 19

United Nation's Day (October 24) 26

Halloween (October 31) 34

Election Day (First Tuesday in November) 44

Thanksgiving (Fourth Thursday in November) 50

Hanukkah (Variable) 57

Las Posadas (December 16–25) 63

Christmas (December 25) 68

New Year's Eve/New Year's Day (December 31/January 1) 75

Martin Luther King, Jr., Day (January 15) 84

Abraham Lincoln's Birthday/George Washington's Birthday
   (February 12/February 22) 89

St. Valentine's Day (February 14) 96

Leap Year Day (February 29) 102

Resources 106

Introduction

Young children can get butterflies in their tummies just thinking about holidays. Holidays are special times for them and certainly for adults, too. Many holidays mean a vacation from school for the children and for the teachers.

Many holidays have traditions that we follow year after year and don't know why we do. In this book we have included several types of holidays: religious holidays, national holidays, regional holidays, and days that the President, governor or states proclaim.

Religious holidays which are included:
> Hanukkah
> Christmas

National holidays declared by the Congress which are included:
> Labor Day
> Columbus Day
> Election Day
> Martin Luther King, Jr., Day

Holidays declared by presidential proclamation which are included:
> Citizenship Day
> United Nation's Day
> Thanksgiving
> Lincoln's and Washington's Birthdays

Others celebrated by tradition which are included:
> Halloween
> Valentine's Day
> Leap Year Day

Holidays brought to this country by recent immigrants which are included:
> Posadas

With each holiday, we have tried to bring you information about the holiday as well as ways to present that information to the children, with activities to reinforce the children's learning.

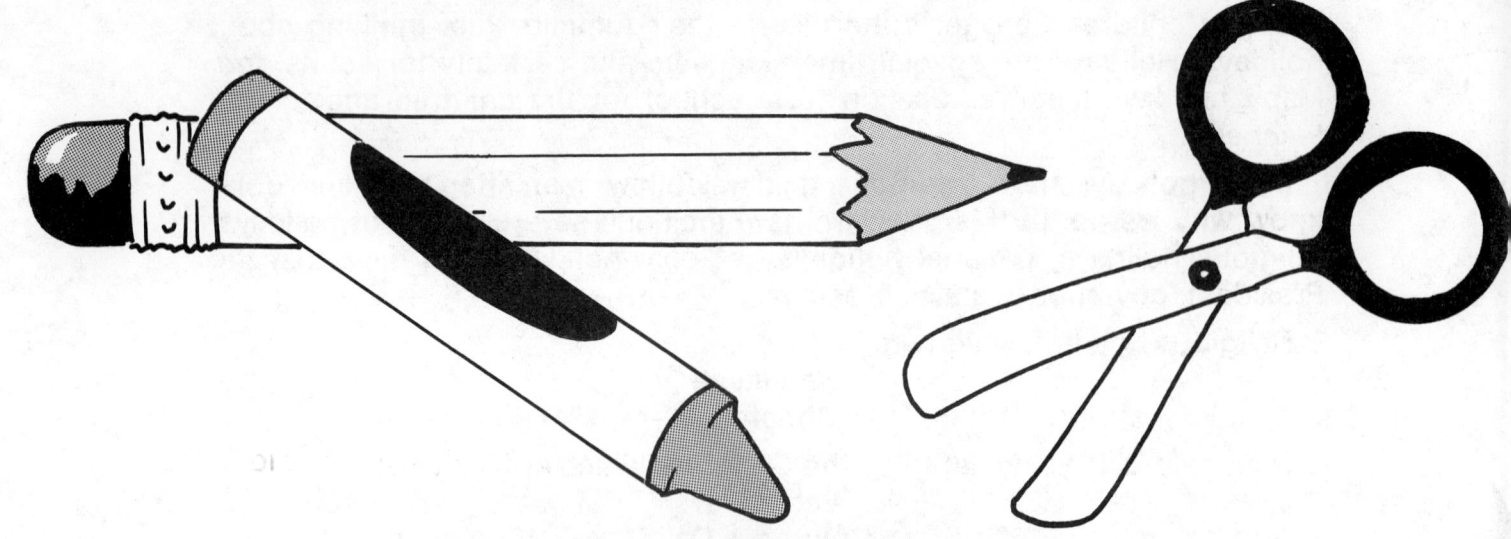

How to Use This Book

Children's Story

Each of the holidays presented in this book has a story devised to present the information about the holiday to the children. The story is presented in large type in order that the oldest of the children in the primary grades might use it for self-instruction. It is hoped that the teacher will present the story to the younger children using the story, the story props, the information presented in For the Teacher, and the method of presentation suggested in Presenting the Story. Each story tells *why* the holiday is celebrated, *when* it is celebrated, and *how* children might celebrate it.

Story Props

Most of the stories have a suggested story prop to use when telling the story. The props include stick puppets, sack puppets, finger puppets, symbols of the holidays, and prop cards. The directions on how to make these appear at the bottom of the page, and directions on how to use them appear in another section, Presenting the Story.

For the Teacher

There is some information about the holidays that does not fit well into the script for the children, but it is information that the teacher might like to know and might like each year's group of children to know. Each teacher will have to judge the children in each year's group and decide what, if any, of this information can be conveyed to them.

The For the Teacher section includes information on how to determine when the holiday is, if it has a variable date, or how to find the date if there is not one on the calendar. Some alternate celebration suggestions appear in this section when religious holidays are presented.

iv

Presenting the Story

This section is presented in two parts, one for younger children in *preschool and kindergarten* and one for older children in *first grade and above.* The information and activities are not specifically suitable for children above grade three. The Preschool and Kindergarten section tells how to embellish the story, how to add further information, and how to utilize other materials in the classroom and tie them into the holiday story.

The Activities section contains at least one reading readiness, reading or language development activity in addition to some simple craft or food ideas to go along with the holiday celebration. The craft ideas may suggest the use of patterns presented but seldom just for coloring. There are suggestions on how to use the patterns creatively. Some of these activities may have to be modified to meet the needs of the different children in your groups.

In conclusion, each holiday is concluded with a Story Picture. These story pictures can be used in a variety of ways.

Take-Home Paper

Each of the children may have a copy of the story picture and color it. At the bottom of the page are some lines. The younger children can use the lines for their names or for some facts about the holiday that are dictated to you and recorded by you on their sheets. These sheets can then go home and children can share their newfound information with their parents.

Holiday Time Line

Color or have a child color the picture and put it up in the room. Start at the left and proceed to the right as you post the pictures to show the various times throughout the year that the holidays occur. If you have a large calendar, reduce the pictures and place them on the calendar.

Class Holiday Book

Color or have a child color the picture and put it into a plastic envelope that fits into a three-ring binder. Let the *Holiday Book* grow throughout the year. Use the lines at the bottom of the page to have the children dictate a synopsis of the story about the holiday.

Big Book

Enlarge each of the Story Pictures. Have a group of children share the responsibility of coloring the page. Children can dictate to you the information they remember about the holiday to have you print on the lines at the bottom of the page. Laminate each page as it is done. Save the many Story Pictures and put them together in a book that the children can read to themselves at any time of the day. Make a cover for the book that is a collage of the many craft ideas suggested in this book.

Little Books

Reduce each of the Story Pictures. Give each child a copy of the picture. Let him color it. Younger children can use the lines at the bottom to write their names. Older children can write or dictate to you stories about the reasons for celebrating the holidays.

Make a special folder for each child to save the pictures in. At the end of the year, make the pictures into a book and let the children bind the books to take home. The covers can be decorated with holiday wrapping paper or in red, white, and blue—national colors.

Labor Day

A Radio Broadcast

Characters:
- Sally Say, Anchor Person
- Paul Play, Reporter
- Clarence Clay, Parade Organizer
- Molly May, Reporter
- Bill Bay, Union Leader
- Jack Jay, Reporter
- Dorothy Day, Mother

SS: Good evening, boys and girls, ladies and gentlemen. This is *The News at Six*. I'm Sally Say.

The top story on this first Monday in September is, of course, local Labor Day celebrations. Our first report comes from Paul Play in the downtown area. Paul, what's happening in the downtown area?

PP: Sally, I'm here with Clarence Clay, organizer of this year's Labor Day parade. Clarence, why a parade for Labor Day?

CC: The parade by the various workers in our city is a way of remembering. By parading, we are remembering the first Labor Day. In 1882 in New York City, Peter McGuire asked various workers to march with him through downtown. The parade was a mark of *respect* for workers.

PP: How many workers are participating in today's parade?

CC: There are many workers from many different jobs parading today. In our times, there are many types of jobs that were not available in 1882.

PP: That's the news from here, Sally, and back to you.

Labor Day

SS: Thanks, Paul. Our next report is from Molly May with *union* leader, Bill Bay.

MM: That's right, Sally. I'm here with Bill Bay, leader of a local *labor union*. Bill just completed the annual Labor Day speech. Bill will you tell us about your speech?

BB: Molly, I reminded the members of our labor union that they had much to be proud of. Labor unions are groups of workers who join together to improve working places. In the past, working places were not always nice. Labor unions have tried to make them better. Labor Day is the day to remember what workers and labor unions have done.

MM: Thank you, Bill, for filling us in. Sally, back to you.

SS: Our final report is from Jack Jay at the local picnic grounds.

JJ: Thanks, Sally. I have with me Dorothy Day, the mother of four children who is here with her children today on a family picnic. Mrs. Day, what does Labor Day mean to you?

DD: Well, Jack, Labor Day is the final family holiday of the summer. It is a time for my children and me to have one last picnic before they return to school. Soon the weather will be too cool for us to come to the picnic grounds.

I know that Labor Day has something to do with workers. But to me it is a day not to work.

JJ: Thanks, Mrs. Day. Sally?

SS: Thanks, Jack. As you listeners can tell, much is happening in our town on this Labor Day. What is happening where you are? In other news . . . .

Clarence Clay, Parade Organizer

Sally Say, Anchor Person

Paul Play, Reporter

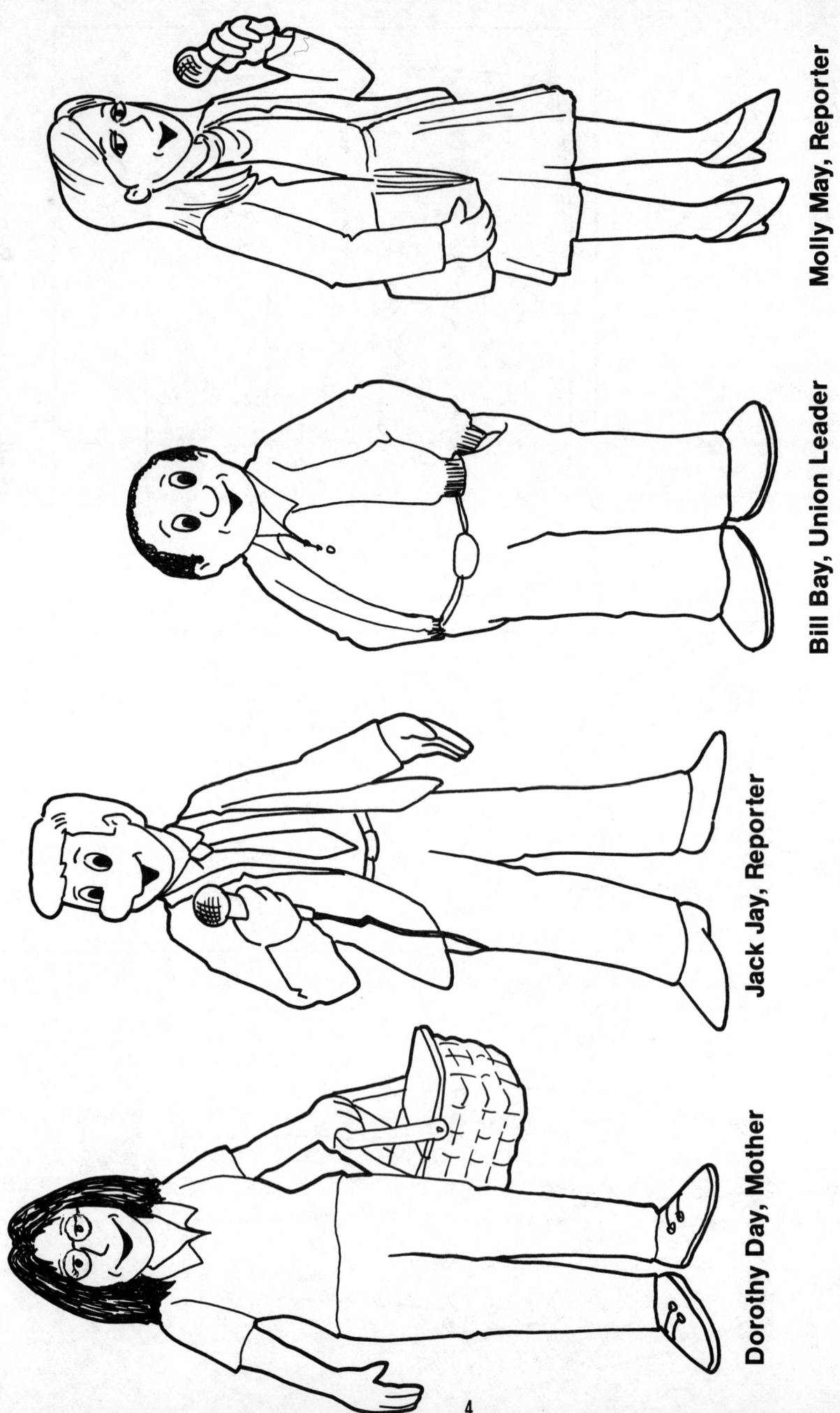

For the Teacher

Many, many years ago on September 4, 1882, Peter J. McGuire was the leader of the Knights of Labor. He founded the United Brotherhood of Carpenters and Joiners. Two years later in 1884 the Knights of Labor passed a resolution making the first Monday of September Labor Day.

The holiday was made official ten years later during the term of Grover Cleveland. He signed a bill in Washington, D.C., on June 28, 1894, declaring Labor Day a holiday, and it has been an official legal holiday ever since.

Presenting the Story

Preschool and Kindergarten

Color in the seven puppets required for this play. Cut them out and glue Popsicle sticks to the backs of them to use for this puppet show. Use your lap for the stage and sit on the floor as you present the play to the children. If you must sit in a chair, make sure that the children are sitting in chairs in order to see.

First Grade and Above

Follow the above instructions. Have close at hand the pictures of various kinds of workers from other units. To make the children aware that the dates of the holidays change, show them when the holidays occur on various calendars from the past.

Alternative Ways to Present

1. Give the script to some parents and have them come in to do the play.
2. Have the older children in the building do the play for the children. Try the upper grade LD class. Let them make props to go along with the play—a picnic basket, parade costumes, a microphone, and have most children wear the hats of various workers.

Follow-up Questions

What kinds of jobs or work do adults do?

What kind of work does your mom do?

What kind of work does your dad do?

How do workers help us?

What kind of work do we do at school? At home?

Activities

Many Hats

Have the children generate a word bank of words that are the names of workers. Place them on a large hat shape. Make a set of flash cards with the names of these workers on them with pictures of the workers on the back. Place them in hats. In pairs let the children read through them to each other.

Helper Chart

If you do not have a helper chart in the room, make one and let the children tell you what jobs there are for them to do in the classroom. Make a sign for each helper and place on a worker's apron—with many pockets. Read *Katy No Pocket* to show how the worker's apron can be used to hold many things.

Guess What I Do

Have the children bring something from home that shows what their parents do at work—a briefcase, a hard hat, an apron, a pencil, chalk and an eraser, diapers, pots and pans, etc. Make sure that they do not show it to anyone until they are ready to guess what the parent does.

Send a note home explaining what you are doing, and ask the parents to explain a bit about their jobs to their children in order that their child may share those work responsibilities with the class.

Goods or Services

Discuss the two types of jobs that people can have, ones that produce goods or ones that provide services—things that people give to us or things that people can do for us. Cut pictures out of magazines of various workers and have the children post them under the two headings.

Goods	Services

Celebration
Labor Day Parade
Music

Choose some march music for the children to march to. Have them practice marching the week before without their costumes.

Band

Drum: Coffee can

Rhythm sticks: Tree branches

Shakers: Saltshakers with beans

Use the rhythm instruments with the marching music the week before the big parade. Do not have the children march and do the instruments together for the first three or four times they march or play the instruments.

Costumes

The children can wear the hats of the workers they represent or make uniforms from grocery sacks for the postal worker, fireperson, etc.

Story Picture

_____
_____
_____
_____
_____

Labor Day

Citizenship Day
A Puppet Show

Characters: Betsy Ross, maker of first American flag
Daniel Boone, early American explorer
Alexander G. Bell, inventor of the telephone
Martin L. King, Jr., leader for human rights

Betsy: (walking on stage) Hello, girls and boys. My name is Betsy Ross. You may know me as the person who made the first American flag. I'm here today, however, to tell you about something else.

Today is Citizenship Day. *Citizenship* is a long word which means different things to different people. I have invited several of my famous friends to join me so that we can explain Citizenship Day.

(Betsy walks to stage left and is joined by Daniel Boone. They return to center stage.)

The first person that I would like to introduce is Daniel Boone. Dan and I lived about the same time but in very different places.

Daniel: Betsy and I were both alive during the 1700's. We both look at citizenship as doing something for those around you. Betsy made the first flag. I *explored* new places for people to live.

Doing something for others is one way of showing your citizenship. Now, you can't make the first flag or explore new land, but there are other things that you might do. Can you think of any?

Betsy: While the boys and girls are thinking, Dan, I want to thank you for dropping by today (both walking back to stage left).

Daniel: Oh, Betsy, think nothing of it. It is always a pleasure to see you. (Daniel exits. Betsy faces the audience.)

Betsy: My next guest is Alexander Graham Bell, *inventor* of the telephone. (He enters.) Alexander, say hello to the youngsters.

Alex: Hello there, young people. It is an honor to be here on Citizenship Day. (Together Betsy and Alex walk center stage.)

Betsy: Alexander, would you tell us about your views on citizenship?

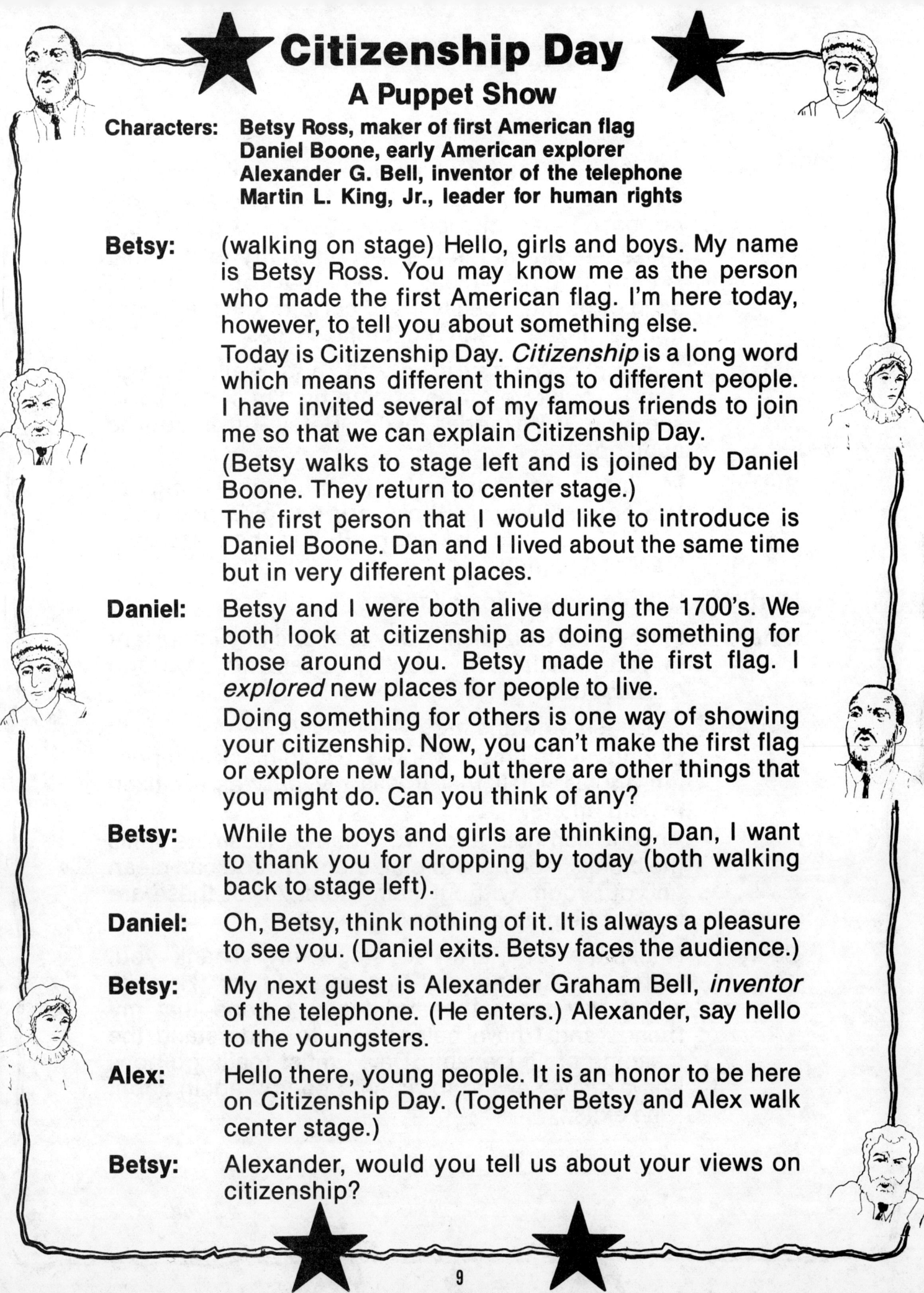

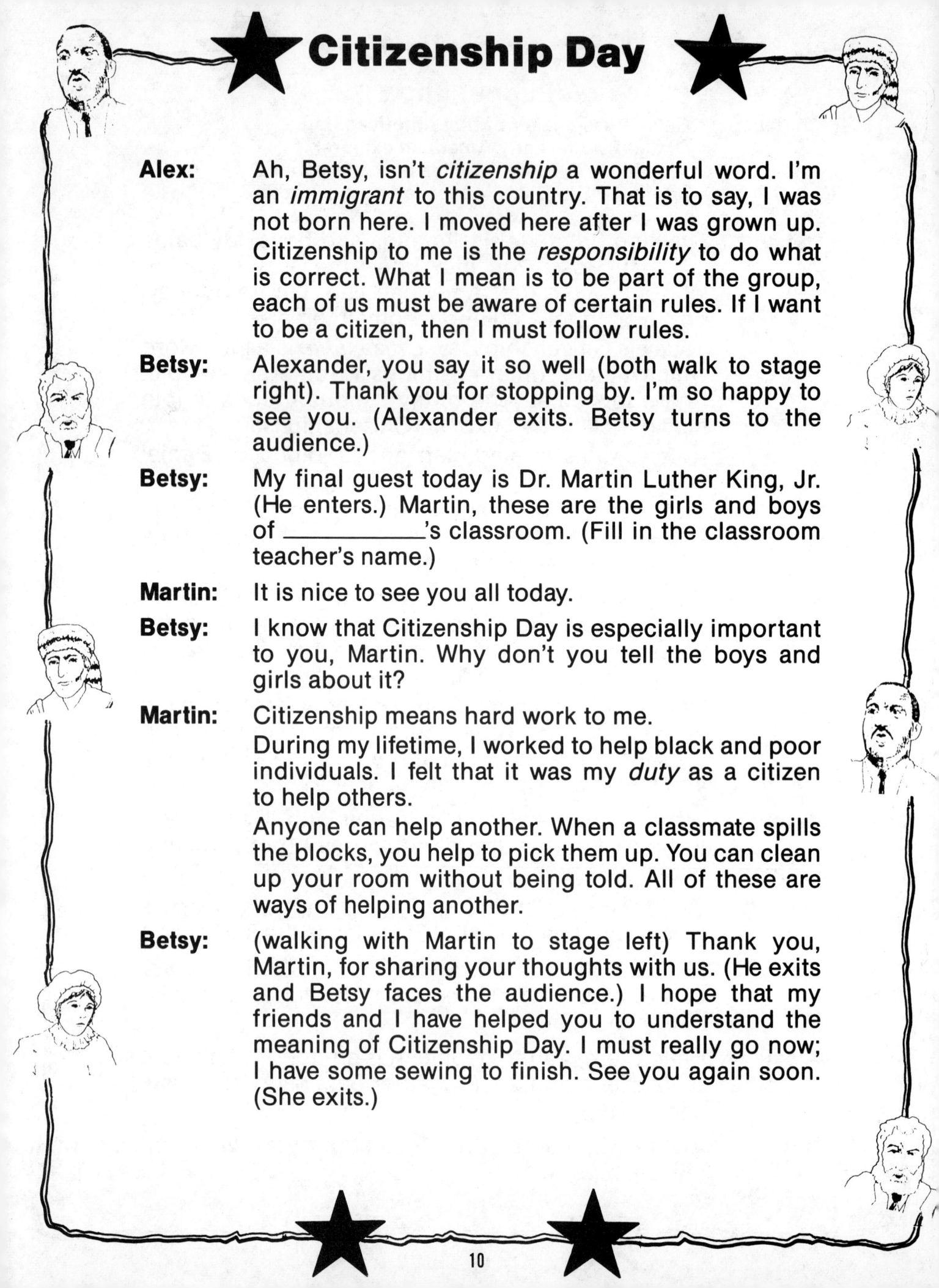

★ Citizenship Day ★

Alex: Ah, Betsy, isn't *citizenship* a wonderful word. I'm an *immigrant* to this country. That is to say, I was not born here. I moved here after I was grown up. Citizenship to me is the *responsibility* to do what is correct. What I mean is to be part of the group, each of us must be aware of certain rules. If I want to be a citizen, then I must follow rules.

Betsy: Alexander, you say it so well (both walk to stage right). Thank you for stopping by. I'm so happy to see you. (Alexander exits. Betsy turns to the audience.)

Betsy: My final guest today is Dr. Martin Luther King, Jr. (He enters.) Martin, these are the girls and boys of _____'s classroom. (Fill in the classroom teacher's name.)

Martin: It is nice to see you all today.

Betsy: I know that Citizenship Day is especially important to you, Martin. Why don't you tell the boys and girls about it?

Martin: Citizenship means hard work to me.

During my lifetime, I worked to help black and poor individuals. I felt that it was my *duty* as a citizen to help others.

Anyone can help another. When a classmate spills the blocks, you help to pick them up. You can clean up your room without being told. All of these are ways of helping another.

Betsy: (walking with Martin to stage left) Thank you, Martin, for sharing your thoughts with us. (He exits and Betsy faces the audience.) I hope that my friends and I have helped you to understand the meaning of Citizenship Day. I must really go now; I have some sewing to finish. See you again soon. (She exits.)

Alexander Graham Bell **Daniel Boone**

Betsy Ross

Martin Luther King, Jr.

For the Teacher

Citizenship Day had a big boost in 1987 with the celebration of the 200th year of the Constitution. Many schools had celebrations with flags, red, white and blue clothing, and parades of their students with Sousa marches, the singing of "The Star-Spangled Banner," and the saying of the Pledge of Allegiance with President Reagan.

September 17 was set aside as *Citizenship Day*, which is the day the Constitution was signed in 1787. *Constitution Day* (September 17) and *I Am an American Day* (first begun by the American Legion in 1940) were combined creating *Citizenship Day*. President Truman signed a bill in 1952 which had been passed by Congress creating Citizenship Day. It is a day when we celebrate being free citizens of the United States, governed by the Constitution.

Presenting the Story
Preschool and Kindergarten

Make the four puppets from the story props. Color each and put a paint stick on the back in order to hold the puppet. Use your piano or piano bench for a stage if you don't have a puppet stage. Have the puppets not in use in a stack for use in the right order of presentation. Stress and explain the italicized vocabulary words for your children in terms that they will understand.

First Grade and Above

Follow the same procedures as for the kindergarten children and in addition, do the following:

1. Show the children the times when the people lived on a time line.
2. Read more about each of the famous friends in the *Founders*, *Inventors*, and *Pathfinders* books of the Famous Friends Series published by Good Apple, Inc.

Alternative Ways of Presenting the Story

1. Read the script to one group of children several times and the stories from other books. Play the part of Betsy Ross yourself, and introduce the three other characters and let the children tell about themselves—not use the memorized script.
2. Present the script and puppet patterns to a fifth or sixth grade class or remedial reading class and ask them to present the play to your children.

Follow-up Questions

We do have rules to follow in our city. The signs tell us about the rules. What rules can you tell me about in our city?

How can we be a good citizen outside?

How can we be a good citizen inside?

Activities

1. Write the word *Be* on the chalkboard or on chart paper. Talk about rules of being nice to others. Make a list of "Be" rules. Have the children illustrate the rules.

    Be
    Example: Be nice.
    　　　　　Be kind.
    　　　　　Be polite.

2. Read the story of Betsy Ross in another source. Show the children a patchwork quilt. Give each child a patch of paper 6" x 6" or 8" x 8". Have each write a citizenship word on the paper and color the background in patriotic colors. Form a Citizenship Quilt for your room.

Symbols

Have the children spend time making symbols that are representative of the United States and of your city.

Flag

Give the children strips of red and white paper and one rectangle of blue. Each should have enough stars to represent the flag you choose to have them make (thirteen or fifty). Glue them onto a piece of cardboard and post them in the room.

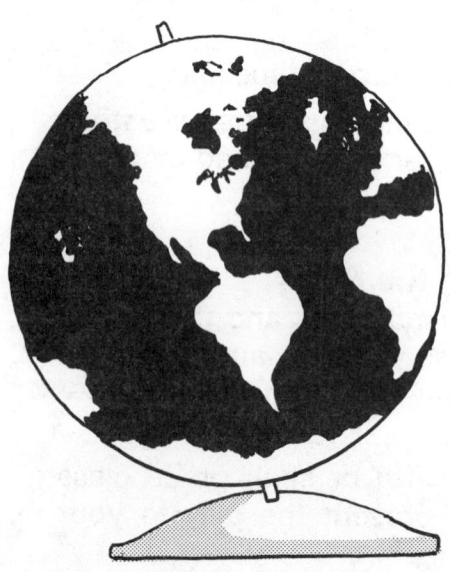

Map

Have the children locate the United States on a map or globe and also locate your state and city. Give them a map that includes the whole Northern Hemisphere and circle the United States in red, circle or color in your state in blue, and draw a black circle near where your city is.

Road Signs

Road signs are signals to remind us of the rules that we are to follow. Use the sheet of road signs on the next page to show the children signs or rules to follow and go on a road sign hunt. Let the child find the colors of the signs and color them in while they are looking at the signs.

We the People

Talk with the children about the Constitution being written as a set of rules for us to follow in the United States. Talk about how the nation is made up of many, many people. Use the outline of the United States map and have the children cut out faces from magazines and glue onto the map, showing that U.S. has many types, kinds, colors of people. Do as a class project or school project.

We the People

Litter Free

Take the children on a walk around the area and look for clutter and litter. Second trip: have them put on gloves and take paper sacks to fill with the litter. Try to keep the area clean of litter for a month.

Litter Posters

Glue some of the litter that is picked up off the area onto a piece of poster board. Title it Please Keep This Off Our Playground. Post where young and old can see them.

Celebration

Present the play to another class. Make booklets of the activities to take home. Make a flag for the cover and a patchwork quilt for the back.

SIGNS

Stop

Railroad Crossing

School

Pedestrian Crossing

16

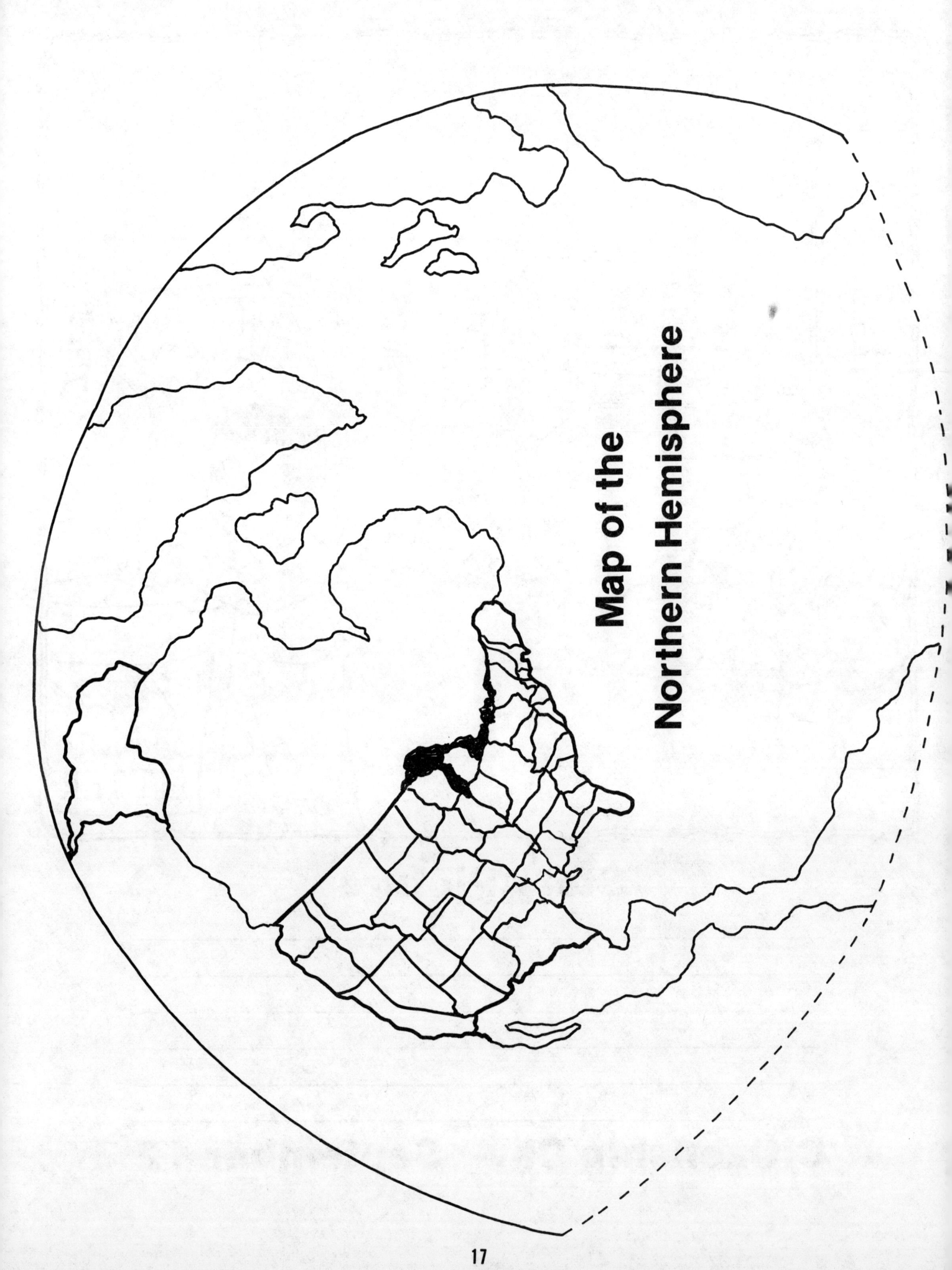

Story Picture

_____
_____
_____
_____
_____

Citizenship Day   September 12

Columbus Day

1

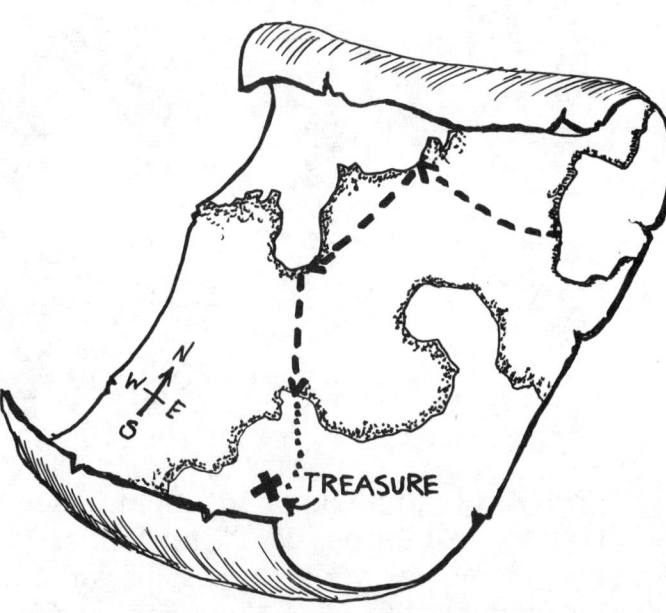

Have you ever gone on an adventure with your family? Have you ever seen a daring performer at the circus? If you have, then you know something about why Americans celebrate Columbus Day.

2

Many years ago, the world was a very different place. There were no televisions or radios. There were no airplanes, trains, or cars. If people wanted to go from one place to another, they went by horse on land or by ship. Most people stayed very close to home.

3

Christopher Columbus was different. He wanted to adventure. He was daring. Christopher lived in Europe, and he was sure that he could get to a place called the Indies by a route that no one had ever travelled. But he needed money to buy ships and to hire men.

4

The King and Queen of Spain, a country in Europe, gave Christopher the money. He bought three ships with the money—the *Nina*, the *Pinta*, and the *Santa Maria*. Some people think he might have had a fourth ship, but we are unsure of the name of that ship. The ships were very small, but they were the best that Christopher could buy for the money.

5

Ninety men were hired to help Christopher—a doctor, cooks, and of course, sailors. Most of the men were not as daring as Christopher, but they trusted him to be the leader.

6

Christopher and the men set sail from Spain on an August clear morning. The *Nina*, the *Pina*, and the *Santa Maria* sailed west from Spain across the ocean. The ships sailed for seventy-two days before they sighted land on October 12, 1492.

7

Christopher was sure that the land was the Indies, but it was not. It was what we now call the Americas—North America, Central America, and South America. It is the land on which Americans now live. Christopher Columbus discovered this land.

8

20

Throughout the years people have remembered Christopher Columbus for his great adventure and for his daring. The first celebration of Columbus Day, however, was not until 300 years after his discovery of the Americas! A small group of people put up a statue of Christopher in a park in New York City.

9

In 1892, on the 400th birthday of the discovery of the Americas, a big celebration was held in Chicago. The Columbian Exposition was like all of the fairs, circuses, and carnivals you have ever seen, rolled into one gigantic party. People came from all over the world to join in the fun.

10

Now, people all over the Americas celebrate Columbus Day on October 12 each year. In South America the children remember the daring Christopher and his men as they crossed the wide ocean in three tiny ships. In Central America children put on plays about the discovery of their homeland. Those of us who live in North America take time to think about what adventures might be ahead of us.

11

In 1992 we will celebrate the 500th birthday of the discovery of the Americas by Christopher Columbus. Can you imagine a birthday cake with 500 candles?

12

For the Teacher

We have celebrated Columbus Day since 1934 when President Roosevelt issued the proclamation asking that October 12 be set aside for the celebration of Columbus Day. It is a holiday that is celebrated throughout the Americas, in Puerto Rico, Central and South America, and Canada. There are also celebrations in Italy and Spain.

The crew members on the ships begged Columbus to turn back. The sighting of birds—a sure sign of land—encouraged Columbus to continue. They sighted land at about 2 a.m. on the morning of October 12.

They found strange things in this new land—naked people with painted faces and bodies and colorful birds, parrots. He took some of each back to Europe with him when he returned with the *Nina* and *Pinta*. The third ship had sunk on a reef near the Bahamas where they landed.

Presenting the Story

Preschool and Kindergarten

This story is presented in a book format in order that you can read it to the children and show them the illustrations. If you choose, you can enlarge the book to use with a large group of children or have individual copies for the children to use as you read.

First Grade and Above

Follow the directions above. Make individual copies of the book for the children to keep. Let them color the book. Locate Spain on the globe and show the children the path that the ships might have followed.

Follow-up Questions

What do you think it would be like sailing on a ship when you could see no land?

What might have happened if Columbus had not discovered America?

Why do you suppose the people did not want to give Columbus the money to go find the Indies?

If you could discover some new land, what would you want it to look like?

Activities

1. After you have read the story to or with the children, have them tell you words that are "Columbus" words (ocean, *Nina*, *Pinta*, Queen, Spain, Indies) and write those on the board. Let them copy them onto slips of white paper in the shape of sails and glue them to straws. These will be the masts of the ships that the children will make.

2. Let the children tell you all the different types of feelings that Columbus felt throughout the story. Starting with paragraph 3 of the story, read the paragraph and have them tell you what feeling words they heard or thought about. Record the words and make a poem about Columbus.
    Columbus,
    Daring and different,
    Happy to buy ships,
    A trusted leader.

Ships

Clay

Have the children mold ships out of clay or play dough. Let them put straws in them as masts. For the more advanced children, let them see if they can make the ship float.

Milk Carton

Give each child a milk carton and cover it with brown paper. The straws can be put in the cartons to form the masts. They will float in the water—and make a mess. If you choose to have them float, don't wrap them in brown paper.

Construction Paper

Give the children a 4½" x 12" pieces of brown construction paper and have them cut off the two corners at the end of the 12" side. Glue it to a 12" x 18" piece of blue construction paper and then glue the straw masts to the boat. Give them 3" x 4" pieces of white paper and let them each draw a person and cut it out to place on the ship.

Celebration

Make a paper birthday cake for the Americas and put it on the bulletin board. Subtract 1492 from the year that it is now: Example: 1988-1492 = 496. Divide 496 by the number of children in your class. Example: 496 divided by 24 = 20 with 16 left over. Have each child cut out 20 strips from a 4" x 6" piece of paper to use as candles. You will have to cut 16 yourself as you model how to cut them out. Glue the candles to the cake.

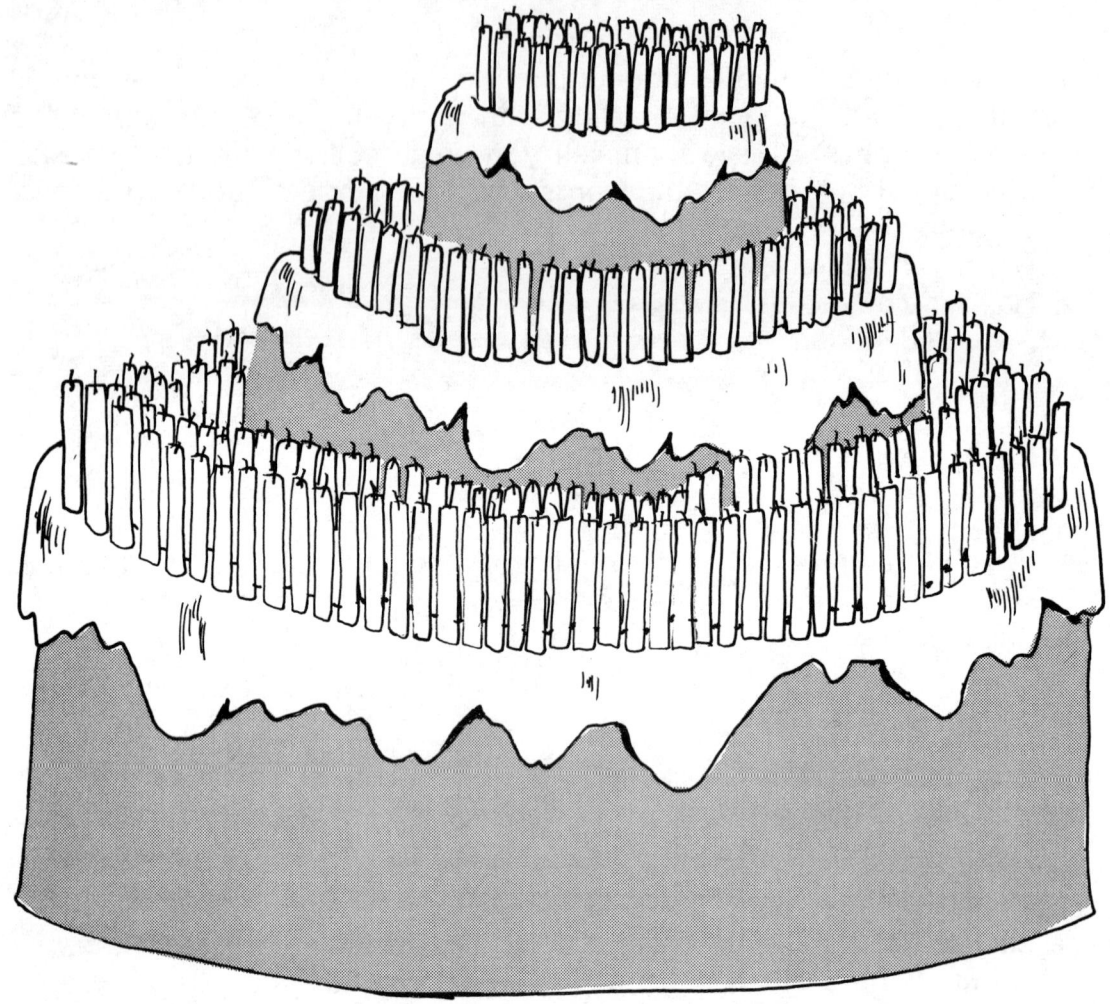

Bake a sheet cake and cut in the shape of the United States. Put candles on it to represent the hundreds, tens and ones—4 9 6. Light the candles as you sing "Happy Birthday" to the Americas.

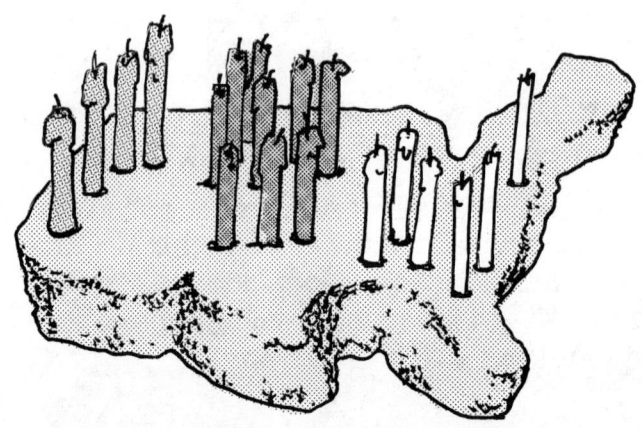

Story Picture

_____
_____
_____
_____
_____

Columbus Day

United Nation's Day
A Puppet Show

Puppet Characters: Chang, a boy from China
Mari, a girl from India
Okon, a boy from Central Africa
Margaret, a girl from England

(All children are present throughout the entire play. Two puppets are on each hand.)

Chang: We are very happy to be here with you today. Let me begin by introducing myself. I am Chang from the People's Republic of China. Mari is from India. (Mari acknowledges the class.) Okon is from Central Africa. (He bows.) And Margaret is from England. (She bows.)

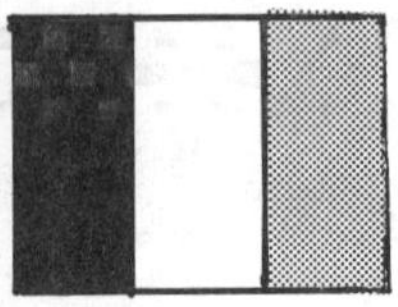

Margaret: We have gathered from homes all over the world to tell you about the holiday we are celebrating today.

Mari: Yes, today is United Nation's Day.

Okon: The United Nations is a place where all the nations of the world may work together to solve the problems that we have.

Margaret: The United Nations was first formed in 1948.

Chang: But it was thought of many years before that by a man by the name of Franklin Roosevelt.

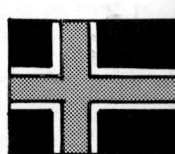

Mari: He was one of your Presidents, by the way.

Okon: The United Nations is important to all of us.

Chang: That's right, Okon. The United Nations provides a place for the nations of the world to talk with one another.

Margaret: The hope of all this talking is that we won't fight anymore wars.

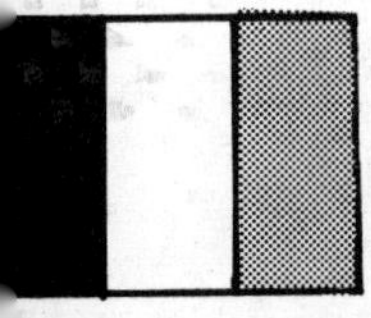

Mari: But the United Nations does more than just talk, Margaret.

Chang: Mari's correct. The United Nations works in many countries to improve the *living conditions* of the people.

Mari: In India, the United Nations is very respected.

Margaret: That is why there is a holiday called United Nation's Day.

Chang: It is a day to talk about the United Nations and to remember how hard the United Nations works to help all of us.

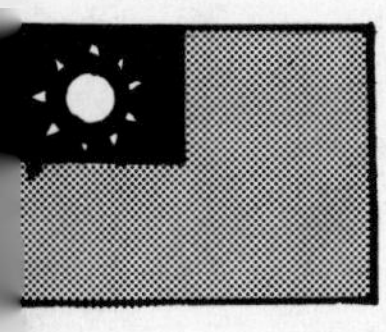

Okon: Why don't all of you join my friends and me. Join hands as a sign of friendship on United Nation's Day.

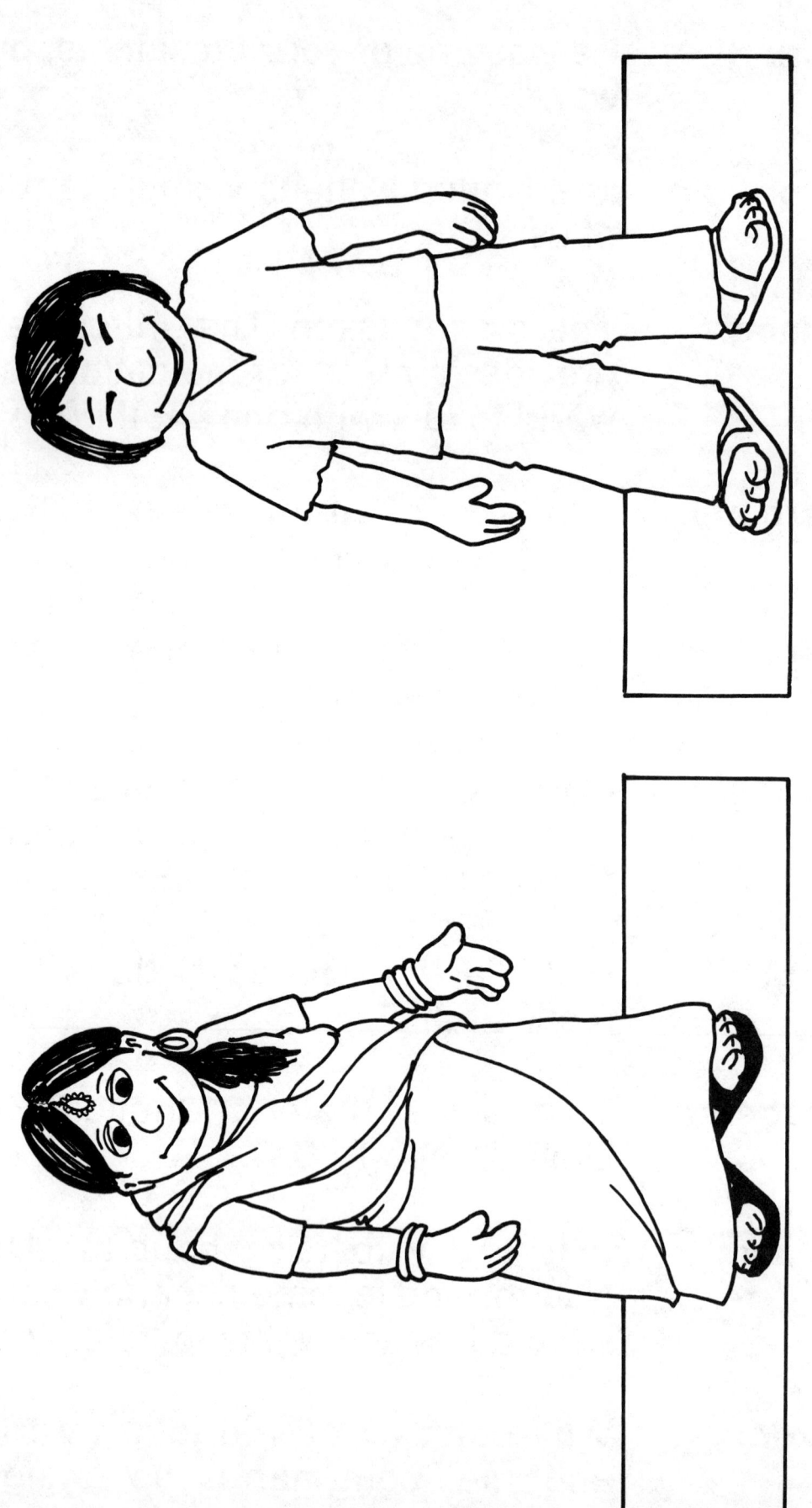

Chang, a boy from China

Mari, a girl from India

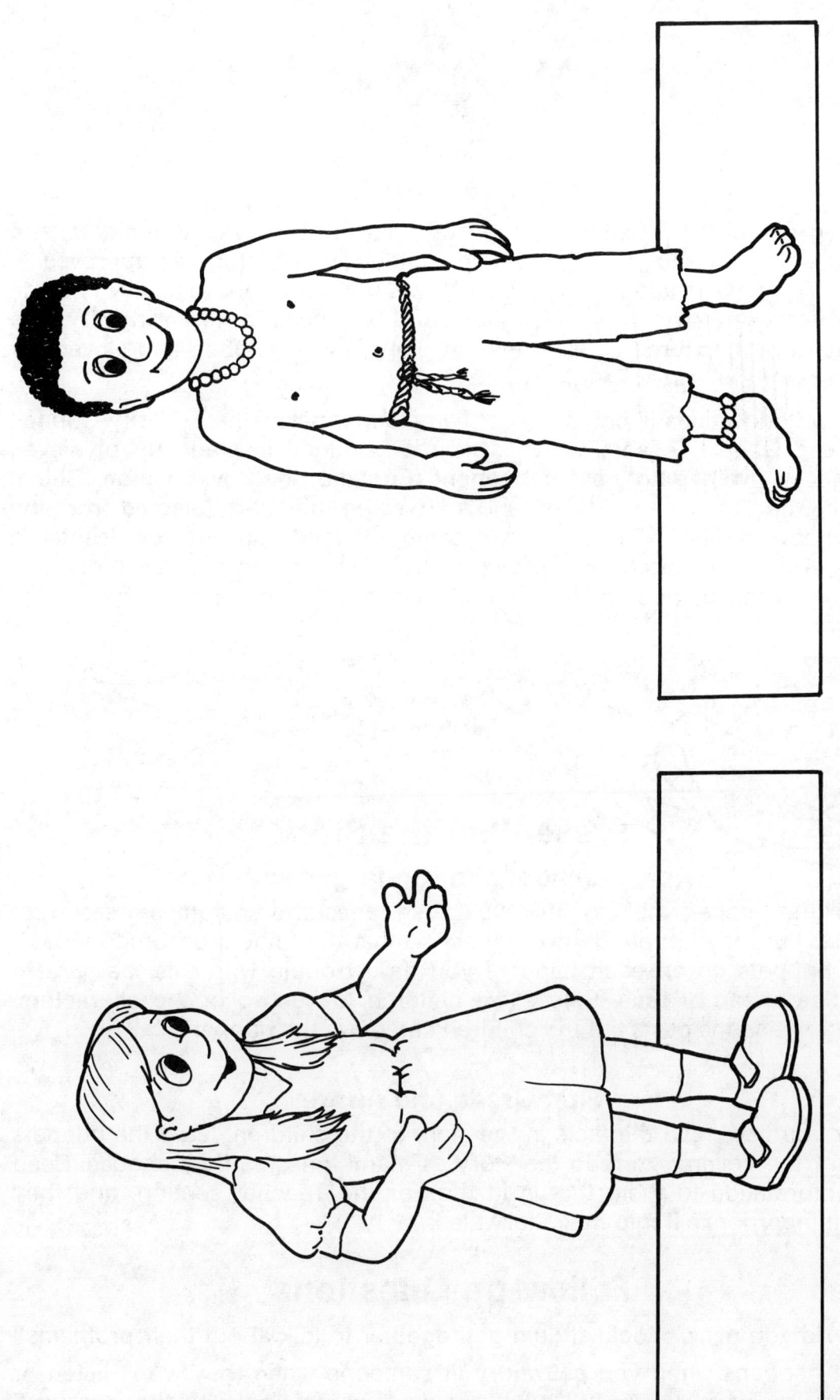

Okon, a boy from Central Africa

Margaret, a girl from England

For the Teacher

During World War II nations of the world saw a need to communicate, and steps were taken to form the United Nations. Its charter was approved in 1945. Three years later in 1948 the UN was first convened. The UN is made up of representatives from 159 nations and is housed in New York City. The group convenes three times a year, in September, October, and November when resolutions are brought before it.

The United Nations is composed of two distinct parts, the Security Council and the General Assembly. The Security Council is made up of eleven members, five of whom are permanent (England, the Soviet Union, China, France, and the United States) and six elected members (elected from the General Assembly). The General Assembly is made up of a representative from every nation that belongs to the UN and each representative has one vote. It is the purpose of the Security Council to keep peace throughout the world.

Presenting the Story

Preschool and Kindergarten

Color the puppets making sure their flesh tones and costumes are correct colors. Put the puppets on two fingers so that the fingers become the feet. Two puppets go on each hand. If you have trouble with this, be sure to practice ahead of time. Select two children to be two of the characters. You can read the parts but the children can move the puppets.

First Grade and Above

After you have read the facts in the story to the children, leave the puppets out for the children to redo the story as many times as they choose. Read the information to them that is in the For the Teacher section, and they might incorporate it into their story also.

Follow-up Questions

Why do you think people should get together to talk about their problems?

What happens when you get angry at someone when they won't listen or let you do what you want? What are ways of dealing with these issues?

What types of things make you really mad?

Activities

1. Write the two words *angry* and *happy* on the board. Have the children tell you what they do when they are angry or happy and record their responses.

2. Make a sheet for them that has "I get angry when _____" on one half and "I am happy when _____" on the other half. Have them illustrate their thoughts and dictate to you their responses. Form them into a class book.

Flags of Many Nations

Use the encyclopedia to show the children the flags of the many nations. Give them a stack of 4" x 6" paper and let them copy their favorite flags from the book. Label the flags on the bulletin board. (Some are easier than others—choose those for the beginners.)

Flags of Many Nations

My Flag

On one of the 4" x 6" pieces of paper, have the children design their own flags using their favorite three colors and their favorite pictures. Glue them to sticks.

Conflict Resolution

Spend time in the group working out problems that the group has. Have them dictate to you the problems that they are having, and you put them on a form entitled "Resolutions." Take the resolutions before the group. After the people having the problems present their sides, ask the group for information on how to solve them. Take a vote and decide what should be done. Ask the warring parties to abide by the decision.

Celebration

Have a parade of the flags the children have made in the My Flag activity. Place the flags in blobs of clay in the front of the class where the flags can be seen. Present "Resolutions" to the group and make suggestions for change. During the closing ceremony, have the children take their flags to their desks.

Flag labels (left to right):
- Flag 1: Orange, Green
- Flag 2: Blue, Red
- Flag 3: Green, Brown, Green, Red
- Flag 4: Green

Story Picture

_____
_____
_____
_____
_____

United Nation's Day   October 24

Directions to the teacher: Be sure that you help the children get the right colors on the flags or ask them not to color them at all.

33

Halloween
A Participatory Play

Characters: Witch—The Teacher
Black Cats—1/3 of the class
Jack-O'-Lanterns—1/3 of the class
Ghosts—1/3 of the class

Witch: (Always speaks in a hushed tone.) Thank you all for gathering on this night of nights.
Welcome, my friends, the black cats.

Cats: Hiss. Hiss.

Witch: Welcome, glowing jack-o'-lanterns.

Jacks: (All make chuckling sounds.)

Witch: Welcome, ghosts.

Ghosts: Boo!

Witch: Tonight is Halloween. We are gathered here just like people from many years ago, with masks on our faces.
Some of us are black cats.

Cats: Hiss. Hiss.

Witch: . . . some are jack-o'-lanterns,

Jacks: (All make chuckling sounds.)

Witch: . . . and some are ghosts.

Ghosts: Boo!

Witch: The masks on our faces are to frighten the spirits that are around this evening. Tomorrow is All Hallow's Day. Tonight is All Hallow's Eve or Halloween. The spirits are gathering. Our masks will keep us safe. The black cats . . . .

Halloween

Cats: Hiss. Hiss.

Witch: . . . and jack-o'-lanterns,

Jacks: (All make chuckling sounds.)

Witch: . . . and ghosts . . . .

Ghosts: Boo!

Witch: . . . are all symbols of Halloween. The black cats . . .

Cats: Hiss. Hiss.

Witch: remind us of the blackness of night. The jack-o'-lantern . . .

Jacks: (All make chuckling sounds.)

Witch: gives us light as we search for the spirits of Halloween.
The ghosts . . .

Ghosts: Boo!

Witch: . . . with their white faces remind us of the morning to come when it will be dark no more.
All of these, the black cats,

Cats: Hiss. Hiss.

Wtich: . . . jack-o'-lanterns,

Jacks: (All make chuckling sounds.)

Witch: . . . and ghosts

Ghosts: Boo!

Witch: . . . are just boys and girls (all take off their masks) who are ready to enjoy Halloween.

Black Cat

Teacher directions: Have the children color the cat face, cut it out and glue it to a paper plate to make a mask.

Jack-O'-Lantern

Teacher directions: Have the children color, cut out and glue to a paper plate to make a mask.

Ghost

Teacher directions: Have the children color, cut out and glue to a paper plate to make a mask.

For the Teacher

Many of us wonder why we celebrate Halloween. Probably we assume that we dress as spirits or ghosts to come back to haunt people. However, if the Celtic celebration is truly the beginning of the Halloween as we know it, it was little more than a celebration of the harvest—typically a Thanksgiving celebration. The Celtics honored the lord of the dead on the first day of winter. They believed that on that day the people who had died during the past year gathered. At the end of the celebration of the harvest, the townspeople gathered to escort these ghosts out of town and wore masks to protect themselves. Fires were used during the celebration in order to lengthen the day and give them light as winter approached.

The tradition of the jack-o'-lantern is an Irish origin. Legend has it that a man (Jack) was far too greedy to get into heaven and couldn't go to hell because he had tricked the devil, of all people. However, the devil tossed him a coal from hell and Jack stuck it in the turnip that he was eating and used it to light his way as he searched for a final resting place.

The only place where Halloween is a national holiday is in Ireland.

Presenting the Story

Preschool and Kindergarten

The teacher is to play the part of the Witch. Young children will be frightened of you as a witch with a mask even if you dress in front of them. When you play the part of the witch, make a pointed hat of black paper and wrap a piece of black cloth around you as a shawl.

Have one third of the children color the cat masks, one third the jack-o'-lantern masks and one third the ghost masks that are provided. Cut them out and glue them to paper plates. Punch holes in the paper plates and put string in the holes. Adjust to the child's head.

Train the children to say "Hiss, Hiss" when you say *black cat*, to chuckle when you say *jack-o'-lantern*, and to say "Boo!" when you say *ghosts*. Practice several times before you begin the story.

In order for the children to get the information out of the story, you will need to do the story several times. Let them trade masks—if you dare— and then proceed to do the story as many times as they want.

First Grade and Above

Follow the above instructions, but have one of the children read the part of the witch.

Follow-up Questions

What do the cats remind us of? The jack-o'-lanterns? The ghosts?

When we see people in costumes at Halloween, who are they?

Activities

Boo! Have the children tell you the words that rhyme with *boo*. Put them on the chalkboard in pictures or words. If you use words, put them into groups according to the end spelling.

Make a witch's pot out of a piece of large black butcher paper. Have the children tell you Halloween words. Write them onto white or orange 3" x 5" index cards. Put them into the black pot so that the children can write, copy, or use them during the season.

Make a spelling list of Halloween words.

ART ACTIVITIES

Cookie Cutter Forms
Use Halloween cookie cutters dipped in black paint to make outlines on white paper. Let them dry. Keep them until the next day and color them in with crayons using orange, white, yellow and red.

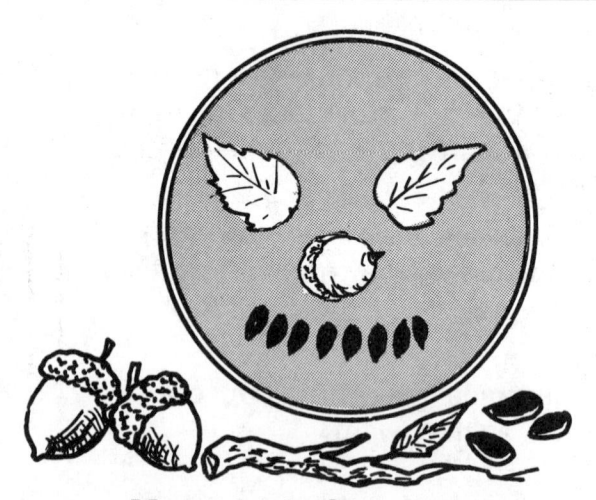

Jack-O'-Lanterns
Cut pumpkin shapes from sponges and let the children sponge paint a set of pumpkins. Let them dry overnight. The next day have the children glue paper scraps to make faces on their pumpkins.

More Jack-O'-Lanterns
Give each child a wad of orange play dough. Have him press it into a plastic coffee can lid. Go outside to hunt for sticks, seeds, nuts, etc., to make the eyes, nose, mouth.

MORE ART ACTIVITIES

Ghosts

Give each child a 12" piece of old white sheet. Place a piece of tissue in the middle of it and gather up the cloth around the tissue to form a head. Tie the cloth around the head. Use magic marker to make the face.

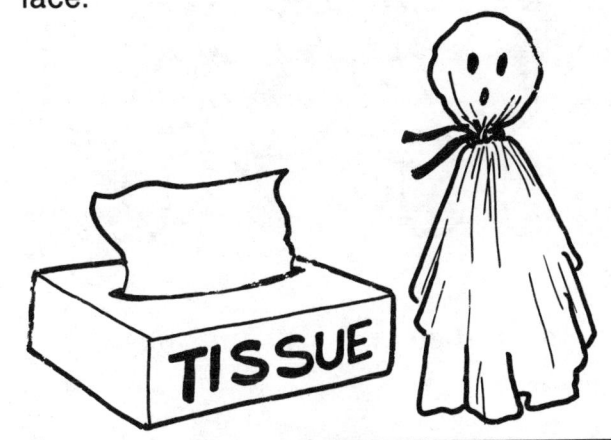

Witches

Give each child a green paper plate and scraps to make a face. Glue newspaper strips around the edge for hair and curl the strips on a pencil to make it ragged. Black paper pointed hats put on the final touches.

Display all the art activities on the branch of an old tree or on a blank tree on your bulletin board.

Celebration

Start with a Halloween parade with the children in costume. Return them to the room for the celebration of trick or treat.

Trick or Treat

Set up centers where the children go to perform their tricks before they get the treat.

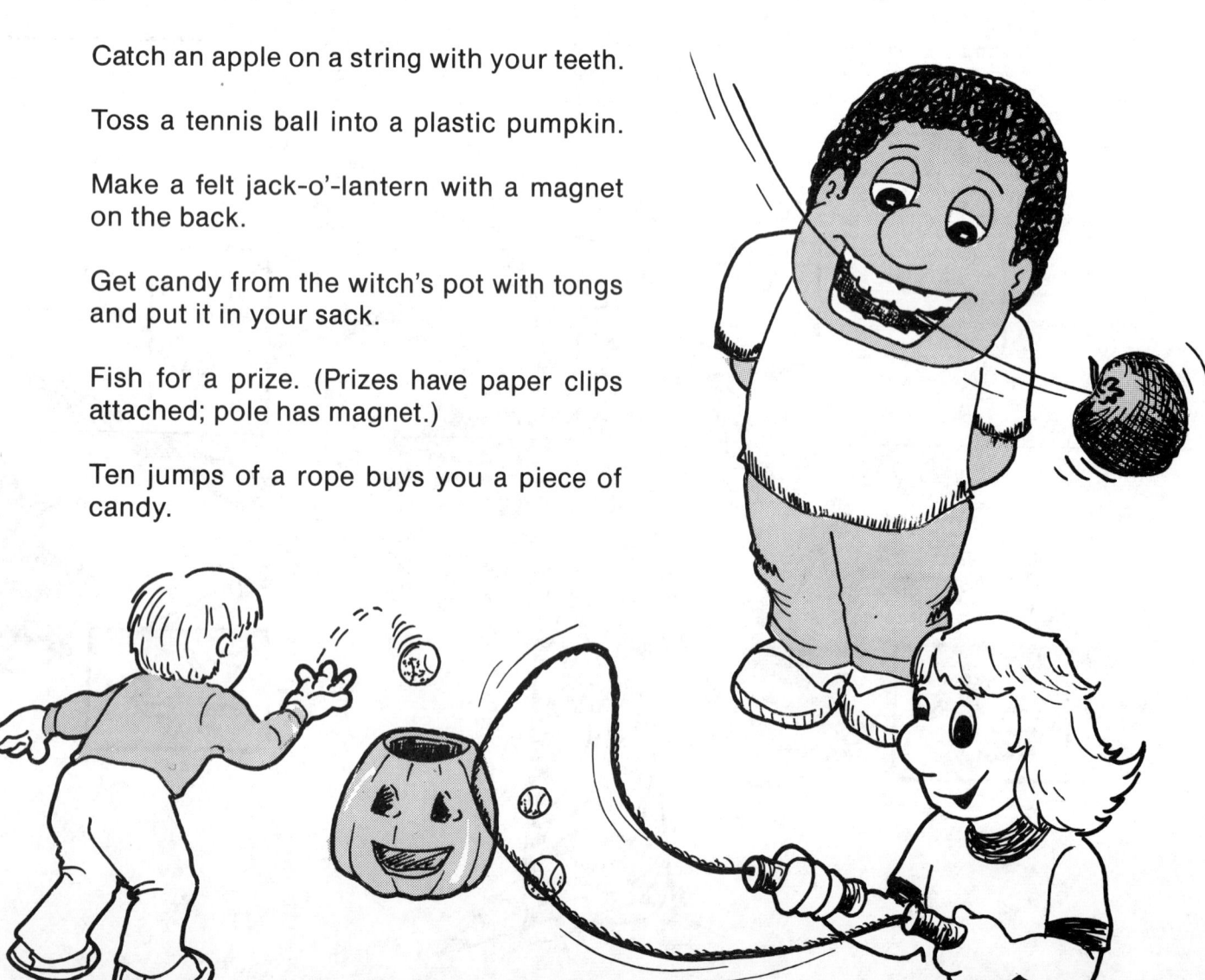

Catch an apple on a string with your teeth.

Toss a tennis ball into a plastic pumpkin.

Make a felt jack-o'-lantern with a magnet on the back.

Get candy from the witch's pot with tongs and put it in your sack.

Fish for a prize. (Prizes have paper clips attached; pole has magnet.)

Ten jumps of a rope buys you a piece of candy.

Story Picture

_____
_____
_____
_____
_____

Halloween **October 31**

Election Day

Children celebrate most holidays. What would a birthday be without presents, a cake and candles? What would the Fourth of July be without fireworks? But there is one holiday that is for adults only. This holiday is called *Election Day*.

Election Day is very important to the people in the United States. It is the day that the people *select* the men and women who will run the *government*. Mothers, fathers, some brothers and sisters, grandparents, aunts and uncles all celebrate Election Day.

You may be wondering what really happens on Election Day. Well, it is kind of like when you push over the first domino in a row and one domino after another falls down. Election Day starts very small and gets big results.

On Election Day each adult over 18 years of age goes to a place called a *polling place*. Many schools and churches serve as polling places. The building you are in now may well be one.

At the polling place, each adult is given a *ballot* or allowed into a *ballot booth*. A ballot is a slip of paper that lists the people who want to serve in the government. In big cities the ballot booth has all of the names listed in a machine and the adult pushes buttons and pulls levers to make a selection.

When an adult pushes those buttons or puts a mark on the paper ballot, he is *voting*. Voting is the big word for choosing between two people. When you choose between grape juice or orange juice at snack time and choose orange juice, you could say that you have voted for orange juice. When adults choose between the two names of people on the ballot, they are voting for a person.

After each adult votes on a ballot or in a ballot booth, all of the votes are counted. Each adult's vote becomes just one of many votes. The election *clerk* counts the number of votes that each person listed on the ballot receives. The person receiving the most votes is *declared* the winner of the election.

The day and month of Election Day is different for different elections. Usually elections are held Tuesdays, but once in a great while, elections are held on other days of the week.

The biggest Election Day is held every four years in November. This is the election of the President of the United States. The date of the election is written in the laws of the United States and says that it must be "the first Tuesday after the first Monday" in November. For this Election Day, everyone is encouraged to go to the polling place and vote. Usually there are millions of people who vote. The TV news is full of reports about the election. Sometimes the people who are listed on the ballots have parties until a winner is declared.

You may want to watch in the newspaper for the next Election Day. You may want to have your own Election Day!

Polling Place

Ballot Booth

Ballot

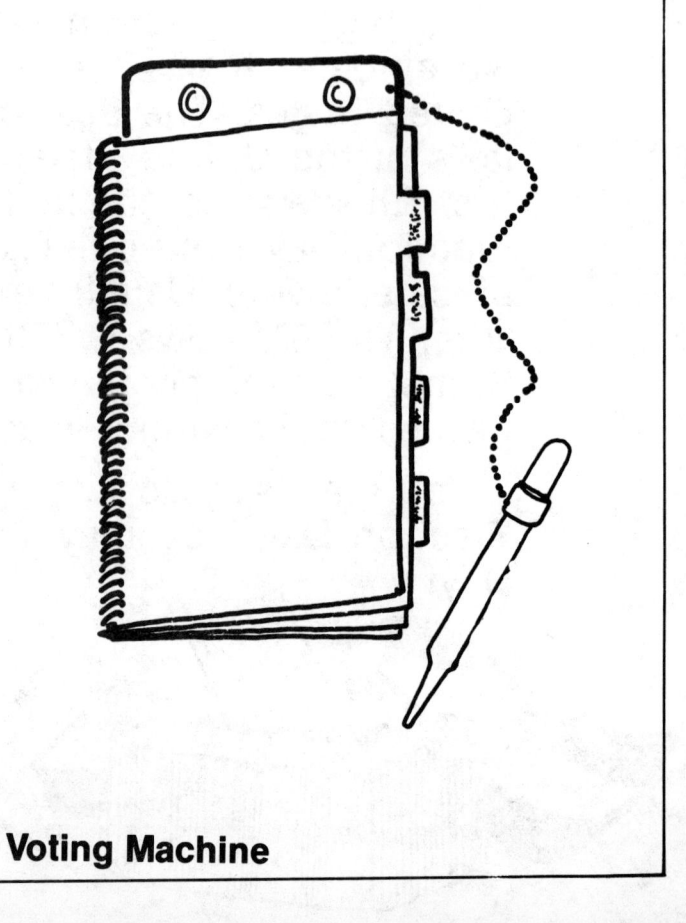

Voting Machine

For the Teacher

Most of the information that is appropriate for you and for young children to understand about the holiday is presented in the story. You might check with local officials who can tell you more about dates, times and places where these occur. Check also to see what types of equipment are used.

Presenting the Story

Preschool and Kindergarten

As you read the story about election day with the children, use the story props as visual aids. Cut them out, enlarge them, reduce them, or make them out of felt.

First Grade and Above

Follow the above suggestions and show the children the first Tuesday in November, which is a common election day.

Activities

1. Visit a polling place the day before or the day after the election.
2. Vote on various activities in the classroom
   - to go outside or stay in
   - to have free play or to color
   - to read one story or to read another
   - to have math or to have science
3. Place the children who vote for one idea in one group and those voting for another in a different group. Match them one to one and see which group has more children. Talk about feelings of winning and losing.
4. Make a ballot booth out of a refrigerator box. Have the children vote on various issues in the ballot booth, using ballots like the ones presented on the next page. Have the children count and recount and record the votes. Declare winners. Avoid voting on class presidents.

Ballots

Directions to the teacher: Cut out each of the ballots separately or use the entire page. Have the children put an x on the one they choose or vote for. If they are old enough, have them count the votes by separating the ballots into two stacks and counting each. Have a recount to check.

Story Picture

_____
_____
_____
_____
_____

Election Day

Thanksgiving

A Play

Characters: Amy, a first grade girl
John, a boy in kindergarten
(John and Amy appear on stage in modern clothes.)

John: Amy, will you hurry up. I don't want to be late today.

Amy: John, I am hurrying. I don't want to be late either.

John: The Thanksgiving *pageant* is going to be great!

Amy: My mom is taking off work to come see it. Thanksgiving must really be an important holiday.

John: Don't you remember what Miss Withers said about it? It's really and truly an American holiday.

Amy: Yes, John, I know the story of how a small group of people called the *Pilgrims* came to this country. They sailed in a very tiny boat called the *Mayflower*.

John: And all of this happened a very long time ago.

Amy: Around 1660. That's before our grandparents were born. Anyway, the *Mayflower* came to shore in a place the Pilgrims named Plymouth.

John: They called it Plymouth because that was the name of the place they had left in England.

Amy: Plymouth is in the state of *Massachusetts*. The winters there are long and cold. The Pilgrims were very hungry during their first winter in Plymouth.

John: Many of them got sick from the cold and from not having enough to eat. They were really happy when spring came.

Thanksgiving

Amy: The Indians showed the Pilgrims how to plant corn and other vegetables.

Oh, there's the bell. We better go put on our *costumes*. The pageant begins in just a few minutes. (Both exit and reappear in Pilgrim costumes.)

John: People sure dressed differently in those days.

Amy: The Pilgrims dressed in white and gray because they believed that clothes should be *plain*. At least when they planted the corn, the dirt didn't show.

John: I bet the Pilgrims were really happy when the corn and other vegetables grew so well.

Amy: That is the reason they decided to have a day to give thanks for the *harvest* of the good *crops*. The Pilgrims invited the Indians to come to a big dinner. They had turkey and duck and deer.

John: All of those lived in the forest *wild* in those days.

Amy: They had corn and the other vegetables they had grown.

John: Dinner lasted all day. The Indians and the Pilgrims played games and visited.

Amy: Each year after that the Pilgrims planned a day to give thanks for their good fortune in America.

John: It just came to me why we call the holiday Thanksgiving. The Pilgrims were giving thanks. Isn't that neat?

Amy: I hear the music for the beginning of the pageant, John. We better get in line. I wouldn't want to miss remembering the Pilgrims and Thanksgiving Day.

John: Me, neither. (Both exit.)

One Boy Doll in Modern Dress
One Girl Doll in Modern Dress

Amy

John

Girl's costume—gray long-sleeved dress which is floor length with white apron and white cap.

Boy's costume—gray trousers and shirt cinched at the waist with a black belt. A brimmed hat of gray with a leather band and buckle in front.

For the Teacher

Thanksgiving is a day of thanks for the harvest, and many countries celebrate a harvest day. For the most part there has been a Thanksgiving holiday in the United States since 1662. At first only the colonists of Massachusetts remembered the day. As they moved to other parts of the country, they took the tradition with them. In 1863 President Lincoln declared a national day of thanksgiving and prayer, hoping that the nation might be able to stop the Civil War through prayer.

Each year there is a presidential proclamation for Thanksgiving Day. You may want to get a copy of this year's proclamation to read to your students or to put on the bulletin board.

Presenting the Story
Preschool and Kindergarten

Make the two paper dolls by coloring them and their clothes and cutting them out. Have everything at your side as you begin to read the script with the dolls. It would be best for you to *know* the script well and not have to read it. The children can dress the dolls when they go off stage to be your helpers.

First Grade and Above

Have the children read the script with you. Each child can have a copy or you can put it on the overhead. After reading the story with them, put the materials and a box for a stage in a center where they can use it and reenact the story. Cut the top and bottom out of the box—and reinforce the sides with a piece of lath the height of the box.

Show the children where Massachusetts is on the globe to make them aware of the place the Pilgrims arrived in the United States from Europe. Then show them where Massachusetts is on a United States map.

Follow-up Questions

What kind of hard times did the Pilgrims have when they got to America?

What did the Pilgrims have to be thankful for?

What things are you thankful for?

What crops grow in your gardens or in your part of the country?

Activities

1. Give each child a brown paper plate or have each paint a white one brown. Put a strip of red in the center for the head. Give them a stack of 1½" x 5" strips of paper and have them cut off the top two corners and clip the edges to make feathers. Glue to turkey.

2. Young children can cut out pictures of things that begin with *T*, glue them on the feathers, and then glue the feathers to the paper plate.

3. Older children can write an alphabet letter and a word that begins with the letter on each feather.

4. Make a thankful book. Give each child a 4½" x 6" piece of paper with the words "I am thankful for _____" written at the bottom. Have each child draw a picture of something he is thankful for at the top of the page and write its name on the blank—or you do that for them. Put it all together into a book and cover with a brown piece of construction paper.

Celebration

Have a Thanksgiving feast. Wear Indian hats, Indian vests, Indian beads, Pilgrim hats and caps, and Pilgrim collars. Eat the foods harvested in the area or traditional Thanksgiving foods and play on the Indian drums.

Indian Headdresses: Follow the directions for making feathers given above and glue to a strip of construction paper. Measure to fit and staple.

Indian Vests: Make vests out of paper sacks by cutting a circle out of the bottom and opening the sack from bottom to top. Cut armholes. Paint with stripes and zigzags and suns.

Indian Beads: Make beads out of salt, flour, water and food coloring mixture. Dry with strays in them. String them into necklaces.

Indian Drums: Make drums out of coffee cans or oatmeal boxes. Cover with paper and paint. Use hands for beating—they are safe and quiet.

Pilgrim Hats or Caps: Draw hats or caps and let the children color them. Glue them to a strip, measure and staple.

Pilgrim Collars: Cut out a large circle with a small circle cut out in the middle. Cut a small pie shape into the circle from the outside and adjust to fit the child.

Story Picture

_____
_____
_____
_____
_____

Thanksgiving

Hanukkah
A Feast of Dedication, A Festival of Lights

Many, many years ago Jerusalem, an important city for Jewish people, was captured by their unfriendly neighbors. The Jewish people were very unhappy and decided to fight to get their city back. They did and they won back Jerusalem.

1

The Jewish people were very happy to have Jerusalem back. They decided to have a dedication ceremony. They cleaned the city and the Temple, their place of worship. When it was all clean, they planned a celebration and called it Hanukkah. *Hanukkah* is the Jewish word for dedication.

2

One part of the dedication ceremony was to light the menorah or candelabrum again. There was only enough oil to light the candles for one day, but when they lit the candles, they burned for eight days. This part of the celebration became the basis for the Festival of Lights and gives Jewish people hope for a bright future.

3

The present-day Hanukkah celebrations recall both the surprise of the menorah and the dedication of the Temple. To recall the surprise of the menorah, the Jewish people light an eight-armed menorah during the eight days of Hanukkah. There is one special candle in the middle (the ninth) that is lighted first and it is used to light the others.

4

On the first night, the shammes is lighted and lights the first candle. On the second night two candles are lighted, on the third night three, on the fourth night four . . . . Each time the candles are lighted, a new candle must be used. Can you tell how many candles must be used to light the menorah for eight days?

5

Hanukkah is a joyous time for the Jewish people. They exchange gifts either at the beginning of Hanukkah or for the eight days of Hanukkah.

Children play with a special four-sided top called a dreidel. On each side of the top is a Hebrew letter. Each letter stands for a word and the four words stand for A Great Miracle Happened There.

6

The celebration of Hanukkah is a very special time for the Jewish people. The Festival of Lights gives them hope for a bright future. The Feast of Dedication or the renewing of their faith gives them strength to continue to be good people.

7

For the Teacher

The Jewish celebration of Hanukkah usually occurs in December. It begins on the twenty-fifth day of the Hebrew month of Kislev. For eight nights the Jewish families gather to remember an important part of their history.

Hanukkah is called both the Feast of Dedication and the Festival of Lights. Both names can be traced to the events over 2000 years that began the celebration of Hanukkah. The Syrians were the neighbors who captured Jerusalem under Antiochus, a Syrian king. The Jewish leader who led the army to victory was Judah the Maccabee.

It takes forty-four candles to keep the menorah lighted for eight days.

Presenting the Story

Preschool and Kindergarten

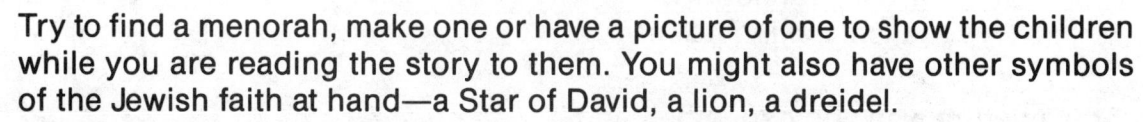

Try to find a menorah, make one or have a picture of one to show the children while you are reading the story to them. You might also have other symbols of the Jewish faith at hand—a Star of David, a lion, a dreidel.

Enlarge the pictures and text, color in the pictures, and read the children the story of Hanukkah. Show the children the menorah and count the candles.

First Grade and Above

Make a copy of the story presented here for each of the children. Let them color in the pictures, cut out the pages, sort them, put them in order by page number, staple them together, and make a cover for the book of blue paper with a menorah or Star of David on the front.

Have the children read the story as part of an investigation into how people celebrate holidays rather than an explanation of religion.

Follow-up Questions

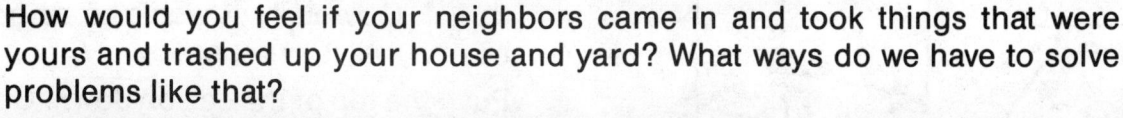

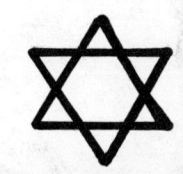

How would you feel if your neighbors came in and took things that were yours and trashed up your house and yard? What ways do we have to solve problems like that?

List eight things that you can hope for in the future.

Can you name other celebrations that have candles or light used in them?

Activities

1. It is a good time to talk about *J* words since both *Jewish* and *Jerusalem* start with *J*. Have children think of *J* words and place them inside a Star of David shape.
2. First grade—Put the word *menorah* on the chalkboard or on a piece of chart paper. Have the children remember that it is a candelabrum, and have them list all the words that they can think of that help them remember "light." The Jewish people believe that the light reminds them of hope.
3. Second grade—Give the children eight strips of paper that they help make into candles. On each of the strips have them write something that they hope will happen in the future. Make them into candles by adding paper flames and gluing to a piece of paper on which they have made a menorah.

Celebration

Let the children eat potato latkes with applesauce, light the eight candles on the menorah, play with a dreidel and talk about good things that they hope for.

Potato Latkes

Potato latkes or potato pancakes are simple to make and the children will have a good time making them for you to fry.

Mix together: raw grated potato
grated onion
dash of salt
pinch of pepper
1-3 tsp. of flour
½ tsp. baking power

If the mixture won't hold together, add an egg or two. Have the children form them into balls and give them to you to cook in hot grease. Flatten them with a spatula. Turn when browned.

Serve on a plate with applesauce and sour cream. Children can choose which to dip their potato cakes in.

Dreidel

You can make a dreidel out of a small school milk carton and a piece of ¼" dowel. Obviously it won't be as good as one that is purchased.

Push the top of the carton down. Cover with brown paper. Make one of the characters on each side (see following page). Push the dowel through from top to bottom. Spin.

Star of David

Let each child make a Star of David by placing two yellow triangles on top of each other, turning one upside down. Make a chain or ½" x 4" strips of blue and white paper so each can wear the star around his neck.

Dreidel Pattern

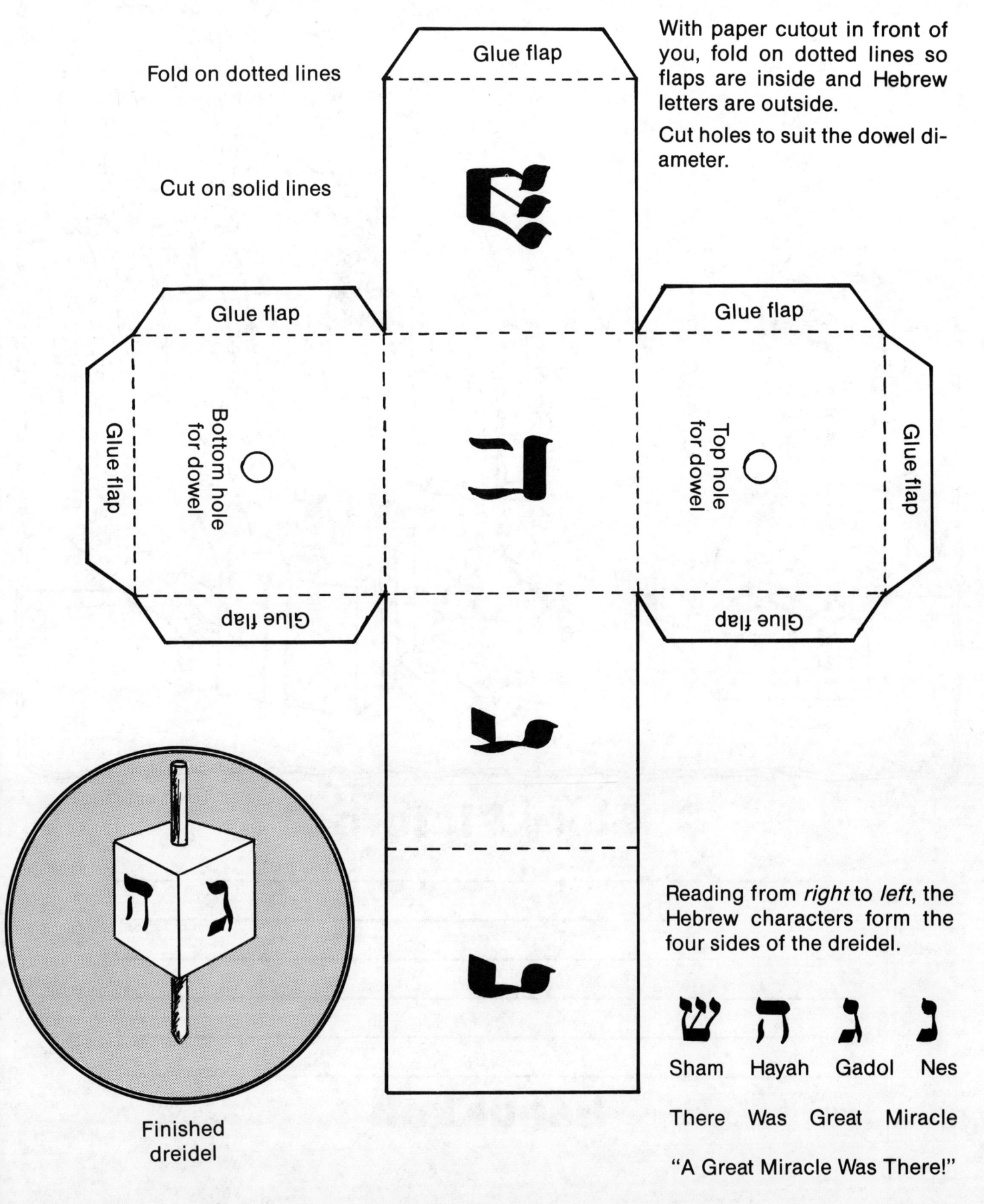

Fold on dotted lines

Cut on solid lines

With paper cutout in front of you, fold on dotted lines so flaps are inside and Hebrew letters are outside.

Cut holes to suit the dowel diameter.

Glue flap

Glue flap

Bottom hole for dowel

Top hole for dowel

Glue flap

Glue flap

Glue flap

Glue flap

Finished dreidel

Reading from *right* to *left*, the Hebrew characters form the four sides of the dreidel.

נ ג ה ש
Nes Gadol Hayah Sham
Miracle Great Was There

"A Great Miracle Was There!"

Story Picture

_____
_____
_____
_____
_____

Hanukkah

Las Posadas
A Story for Children

Las Posadas is celebrated for 8 [night]s just before Christmas. Hispanic [family]s first celebrated Las Posadas. Now many [family]s celebrate this holiday.

Las Posadas means [house]. The holiday reminds us of the journey of [Mary] and [Joseph] to Bethlehem. On this journey [Mary] and [Joseph] sought [house] each [night]. When [Mary] and [Joseph] reached Bethlehem, the innkeeper told [Mary] and [Joseph] that the [inn] was full. [Mary] and [Joseph] found [house] in the [stable] or barn.

During the [night]s of Las Posadas, [family]s seek [house] in a neighbor's home. At first the neighbor tells the [family]s that the house is full. Just like the innkeeper told [Mary] and [Joseph] that the [inn] was full. As the [family]s turn away, the neighbor asks the [family]s to stay. Then the neighbor and the [family]s celebrate with a party.

A major part of the party is the breaking of the 🪅.

The 👦S and 👧S gather in a ⭕. The 🪅, a clay 🏺 filled with 🍭 and 🧸, is hung from the ceiling. One 👦 or 👧 is blindfolded. Then the 👦 or 👧 hits at the 🪅 with a stick. Each 👦 and 👧 is given a chance to hit at the 🪅 until it breaks. Then the 👦S and 👧S enjoy the 🍭 and 🧸.

Las Posadas is celebrated the same way each 🌙. 👨‍👩‍👧S ask neighbors for 🏠 just like 🙏 and 🙏 did. The 👨‍👩‍👧S are remembering the 🌙 of 🙏 and 🙏. The last 🌙 of Las Posadas is Christmas Eve when 🙏 and 🙏 found 🏠 in the 🏚 where the 👶 was born.

For the Teacher

Las Posadas translates from Spanish to mean shelter or lodging. In Mexico, a religious ceremony precedes the party. The community assembles at the church where statues of Mary and Joseph are presented to the family seeking shelter. The family members carry these statues as they go from home to home. Traditionally, a family asks for entrance to the home three times before the neighbor lets them in.

Presenting the Story

Preschool and Kindergarten

This story has no props with it. Props could be made from the pictures in the rebus story.

When working with very young children, it is suggested that you enlarge the page to a ledger-sized page, color in the pictures, and then use a pointer as you read the story to the children. When you come to a picture, they can "read" the word with you. They may need some coaxing at the beginning and may choose to read it through many times in the group and more times alone—with the pointer, of course. Make smaller copies for them to take home.

First Grade and Above

The reading level in this story is not above the second grade. However, some of the children will be unable to read it by themselves. Present the story to the children as a group—possibly as suggested for the preschoolers and kindergartners. Let the children read it to each other and color the pictures.

Activities

Make several copies of the pictures below for each child. Let the children write their own renditions of the story using the pictures.

eight · night · family · shelter · stable

Mary · Joseph · inn · piñata · circle

pot · candy · girl · boy · toys · Baby Jesus

Write the words from the story on a chart. Place the pictures beside the words. Leave pencils and a stack of 4" x 6" paper on the writing table and let the children copy the pictures and the words to make their own set of flash cards for reading.

Celebration

Have children act out the story, selecting three children to be the traveling family and three others be the neighbors living next door. Have the children knock at the door and be turned away. Just as they turn away, have the neighbors invite them in and "throw a party."

Houses

Have the children design 4' x 4' butcher paper into houses that are flat-topped. Outline windows and doors with black tempera. Let it dry.
Color the house, windows and doors with paint or crayons.
Tape the house fronts up on the front of a set of two desks or on the front of a table to use as the house for the neighbors and the travelers.

Manners

If you have had small children for neighbors, you know that they must learn to knock and not to just walk right in and make themselves comfortable. This is a great time to study those knocking manners and also to stress not going to the houses of strangers.

Approach the door.
Knock on the door.
Wait.
Neighbors answer door and say they are busy now.
Children turn to leave.
Neighbors invite them in.
Children say thank you.

Breaking the Piñata

Piñatas are both fun and dangerous in a classroom that is not well-behaved and structured. Children need to be in a large circle in order not to be hit with the swings.

Piñata

Piñatas are available in most import stores. If you cannot find one in your area, make a small one out of a large balloon. Cover it with papier-mâché of bright colors of tissue paper. Let it dry for a week or so. Hang it from the ceiling.

Story Picture

_____
_____
_____
_____
_____

Las Posadas   December 16-25

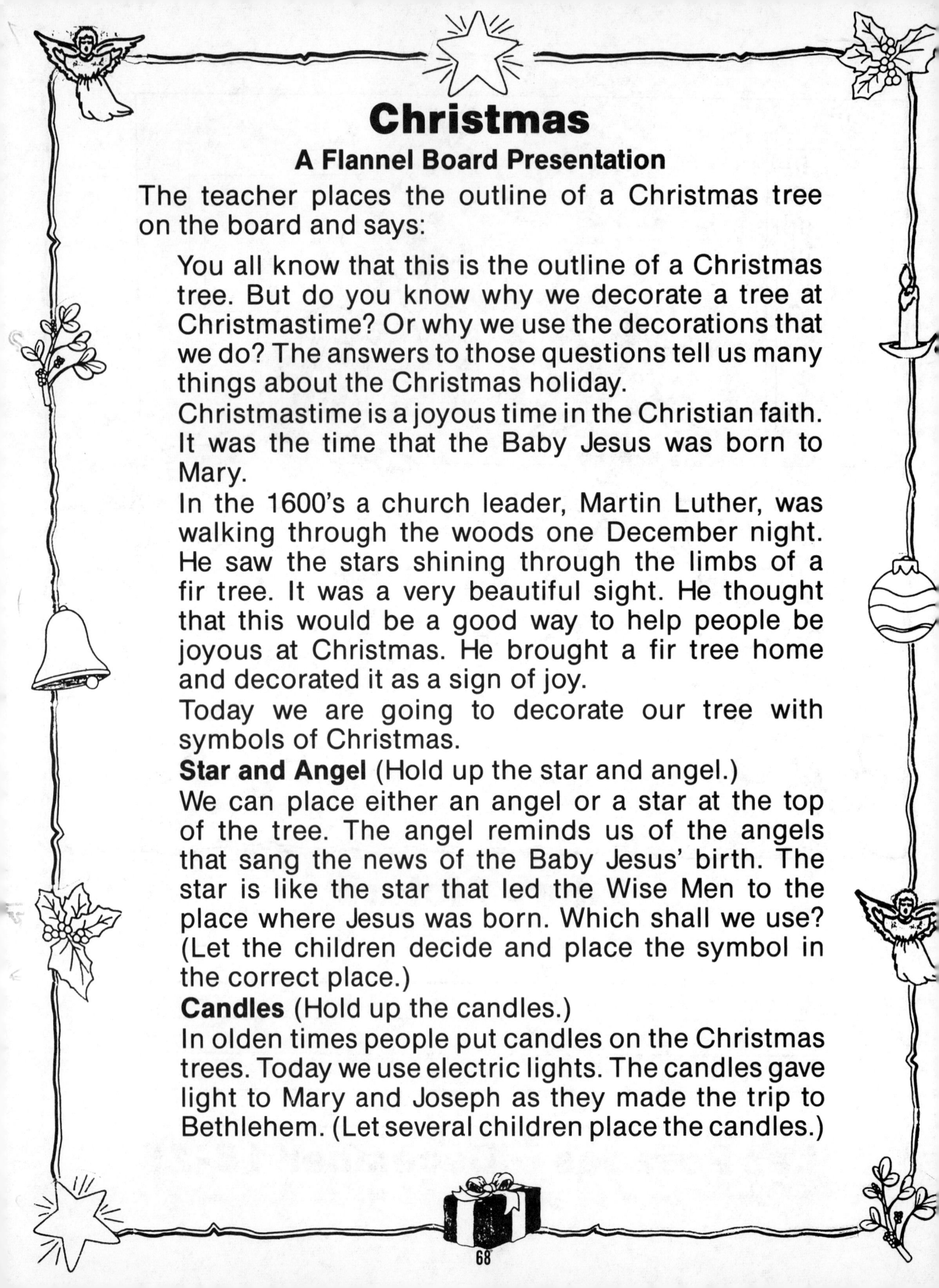

Christmas
A Flannel Board Presentation

The teacher places the outline of a Christmas tree on the board and says:

You all know that this is the outline of a Christmas tree. But do you know why we decorate a tree at Christmastime? Or why we use the decorations that we do? The answers to those questions tell us many things about the Christmas holiday.

Christmastime is a joyous time in the Christian faith. It was the time that the Baby Jesus was born to Mary.

In the 1600's a church leader, Martin Luther, was walking through the woods one December night. He saw the stars shining through the limbs of a fir tree. It was a very beautiful sight. He thought that this would be a good way to help people be joyous at Christmas. He brought a fir tree home and decorated it as a sign of joy.

Today we are going to decorate our tree with symbols of Christmas.

Star and Angel (Hold up the star and angel.)

We can place either an angel or a star at the top of the tree. The angel reminds us of the angels that sang the news of the Baby Jesus' birth. The star is like the star that led the Wise Men to the place where Jesus was born. Which shall we use? (Let the children decide and place the symbol in the correct place.)

Candles (Hold up the candles.)

In olden times people put candles on the Christmas trees. Today we use electric lights. The candles gave light to Mary and Joseph as they made the trip to Bethlehem. (Let several children place the candles.)

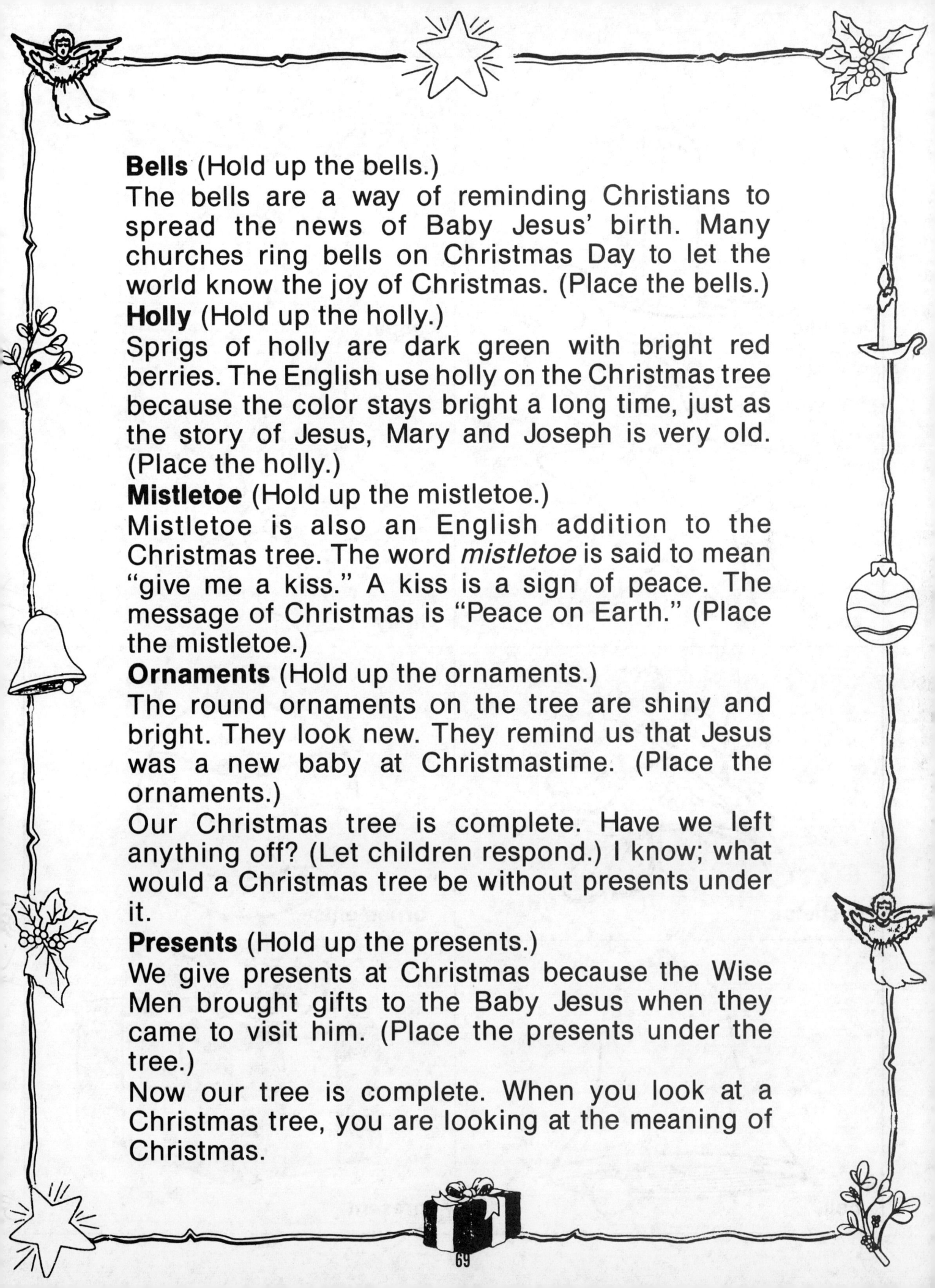

Bells (Hold up the bells.)
The bells are a way of reminding Christians to spread the news of Baby Jesus' birth. Many churches ring bells on Christmas Day to let the world know the joy of Christmas. (Place the bells.)
Holly (Hold up the holly.)
Sprigs of holly are dark green with bright red berries. The English use holly on the Christmas tree because the color stays bright a long time, just as the story of Jesus, Mary and Joseph is very old. (Place the holly.)
Mistletoe (Hold up the mistletoe.)
Mistletoe is also an English addition to the Christmas tree. The word *mistletoe* is said to mean "give me a kiss." A kiss is a sign of peace. The message of Christmas is "Peace on Earth." (Place the mistletoe.)
Ornaments (Hold up the ornaments.)
The round ornaments on the tree are shiny and bright. They look new. They remind us that Jesus was a new baby at Christmastime. (Place the ornaments.)
Our Christmas tree is complete. Have we left anything off? (Let children respond.) I know; what would a Christmas tree be without presents under it.
Presents (Hold up the presents.)
We give presents at Christmas because the Wise Men brought gifts to the Baby Jesus when they came to visit him. (Place the presents under the tree.)
Now our tree is complete. When you look at a Christmas tree, you are looking at the meaning of Christmas.

candle	angel
star	holly
mistletoe	ornaments
bell	present

Tree Pattern

For the Teacher

Christmas is a holiday that many of us cannot officially celebrate in the public schools. We have tried to present the story here as history and symbols of remembrance rather that beliefs in the Christian religion. If you are in a school where you can teach the religion with the story, please do. If you are not, please follow our guidelines as carefully as possible. In fact, you might even check with administrators before you begin.

Presenting the Story

Preschool and Kindergarten

Make a large tree out of green felt in the shape of a Christmas tree. As you tell the story, make sure that each child gets an ornament to put on the tree. If you choose to use the tree and ornaments as an Advent calendar, make enough for each day before Christmas.

Pass out an ornament to each of the children. As you tell about their ornaments, have them come up to the flannel board and place their ornaments on the tree.

First Grade and Above

Give each group of children an ornament to decorate and the information to learn about their ornament.

Bring the children to the circle and have them sit on the floor in the order that their ornaments are presented in the story. As each ornament is presented, have the student tell about it and place it on the tree.

Use this as a presentation for a Christmas party for the parents.

Follow-up Questions

Hold up each of the ornaments. Ask what each reminds us of.

Hold up traffic signs (found in Citizenship unit). Ask what the signs tell us.

Activities

1. Enlarge a copy of the Story Props and post on the bulletin board.
   Fold a 9" x 12" piece of paper into eight boxes.
   Have children copy the words and pictures into the boxes.
   On the back children can make other decorations they know about. You might look up their origins with them. Try candy cane, Santa, wreath, creche, etc.

2. Make a large Christmas tree out of green poster board. Write the Christmas words on the chart in black magic marker. Overnight, without the child there, cover the words with glue and spread glitter. Makes a shiny word bank.

Individual Advent Calendars

Make several copies of the Story Prop page.

Cut up the boxes and put the different ornaments into separate piles and boxes.

Let each child choose 24 ornaments and 1 special one for the 25th.

Cut a large tree for each child out of poster board or felt. Let him put 25 Velcro tabs on.

Let the children color the ornaments and put Velcro tabs on the back of each.

Make an envelope for the ornaments.

Celebration

A Play

Present the information about the ornaments in a little play with the children.

What to Eat

Serve angel food cake with candles.

When to Eat

Ring the bell to tell about Christmas and then eat.

What to Wear

Make wreaths of holly or mistletoe—green leaves glued together onto a circle. Paper punch red berries to glue on. Place them on the head as crowns and then use as wreaths for doors. Make a star for each child to show that he is a superstar.

What to Give as Presents

Let children make wrapping paper by using cookie cutters dipped in paint to make patterns on white tissue paper.

Make gifts for parents—and let the children wrap them themselves.

ART ACTIVITIES

Chip Off the Old Block

A picture of the child glued to a block of sanded wood.

Pencil Holders

Juice cans covered with tissue paper.

Portraits

A traced shadow of the child in black paper on white.

Christmas Villages

Houses made of small boxes decorated for Christmas.

Wreaths

Glue pinecones to cardboard. Tie red bow at bottom.

Story Picture

_____
_____
_____
_____
_____

Christmas **December 25**

New Year's Eve New Year's Day

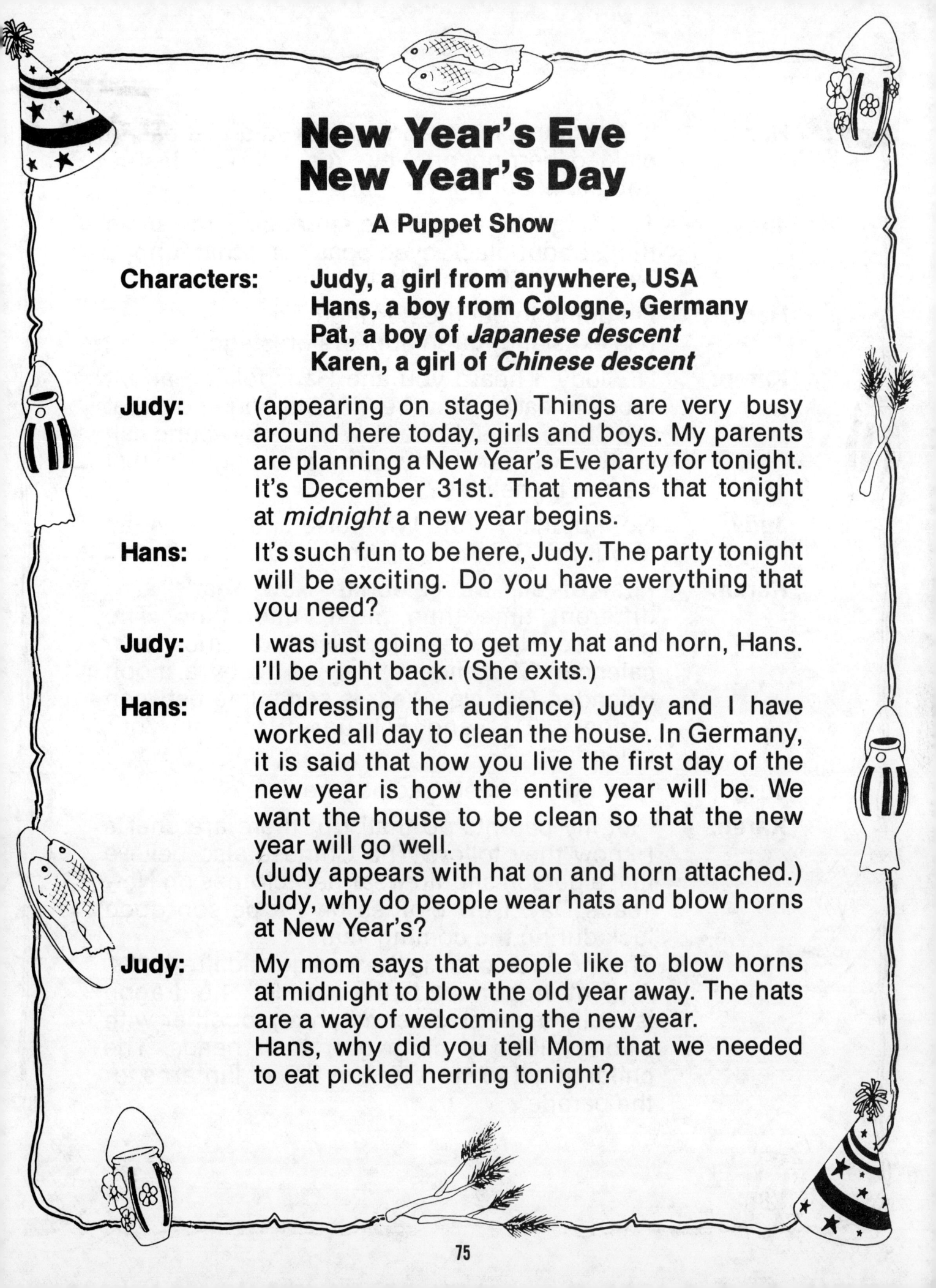

A Puppet Show

Characters: Judy, a girl from anywhere, USA
Hans, a boy from Cologne, Germany
Pat, a boy of *Japanese descent*
Karen, a girl of *Chinese descent*

Judy: (appearing on stage) Things are very busy around here today, girls and boys. My parents are planning a New Year's Eve party for tonight. It's December 31st. That means that tonight at *midnight* a new year begins.

Hans: It's such fun to be here, Judy. The party tonight will be exciting. Do you have everything that you need?

Judy: I was just going to get my hat and horn, Hans. I'll be right back. (She exits.)

Hans: (addressing the audience) Judy and I have worked all day to clean the house. In Germany, it is said that how you live the first day of the new year is how the entire year will be. We want the house to be clean so that the new year will go well.
(Judy appears with hat on and horn attached.) Judy, why do people wear hats and blow horns at New Year's?

Judy: My mom says that people like to blow horns at midnight to blow the old year away. The hats are a way of welcoming the new year.
Hans, why did you tell Mom that we needed to eat pickled herring tonight?

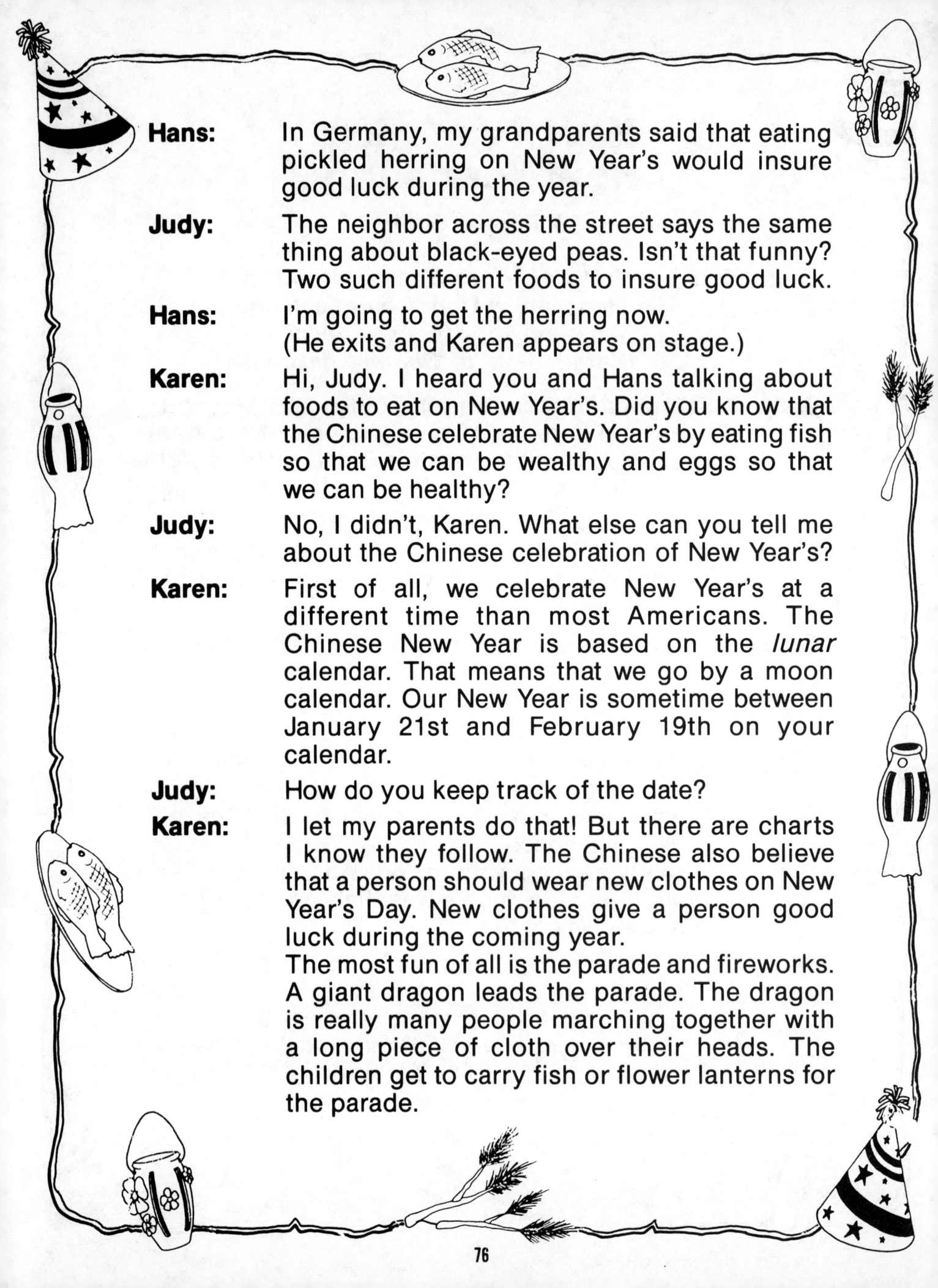

Hans: In Germany, my grandparents said that eating pickled herring on New Year's would insure good luck during the year.

Judy: The neighbor across the street says the same thing about black-eyed peas. Isn't that funny? Two such different foods to insure good luck.

Hans: I'm going to get the herring now.
(He exits and Karen appears on stage.)

Karen: Hi, Judy. I heard you and Hans talking about foods to eat on New Year's. Did you know that the Chinese celebrate New Year's by eating fish so that we can be wealthy and eggs so that we can be healthy?

Judy: No, I didn't, Karen. What else can you tell me about the Chinese celebration of New Year's?

Karen: First of all, we celebrate New Year's at a different time than most Americans. The Chinese New Year is based on the *lunar* calendar. That means that we go by a moon calendar. Our New Year is sometime between January 21st and February 19th on your calendar.

Judy: How do you keep track of the date?

Karen: I let my parents do that! But there are charts I know they follow. The Chinese also believe that a person should wear new clothes on New Year's Day. New clothes give a person good luck during the coming year.
The most fun of all is the parade and fireworks. A giant dragon leads the parade. The dragon is really many people marching together with a long piece of cloth over their heads. The children get to carry fish or flower lanterns for the parade.

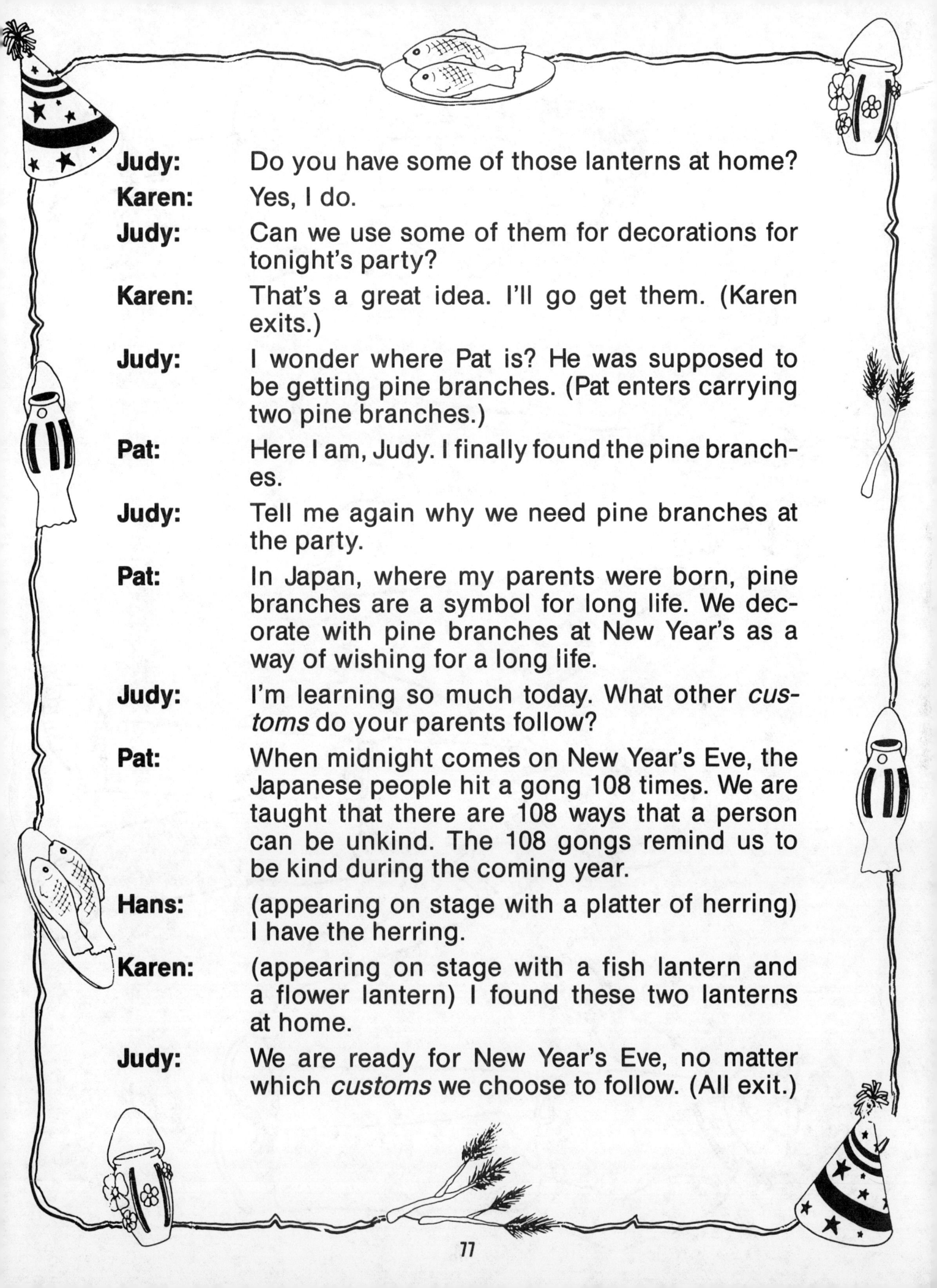

Judy:	Do you have some of those lanterns at home?
Karen:	Yes, I do.
Judy:	Can we use some of them for decorations for tonight's party?
Karen:	That's a great idea. I'll go get them. (Karen exits.)
Judy:	I wonder where Pat is? He was supposed to be getting pine branches. (Pat enters carrying two pine branches.)
Pat:	Here I am, Judy. I finally found the pine branches.
Judy:	Tell me again why we need pine branches at the party.
Pat:	In Japan, where my parents were born, pine branches are a symbol for long life. We decorate with pine branches at New Year's as a way of wishing for a long life.
Judy:	I'm learning so much today. What other *customs* do your parents follow?
Pat:	When midnight comes on New Year's Eve, the Japanese people hit a gong 108 times. We are taught that there are 108 ways that a person can be unkind. The 108 gongs remind us to be kind during the coming year.
Hans:	(appearing on stage with a platter of herring) I have the herring.
Karen:	(appearing on stage with a fish lantern and a flower lantern) I found these two lanterns at home.
Judy:	We are ready for New Year's Eve, no matter which *customs* we choose to follow. (All exit.)

Karen

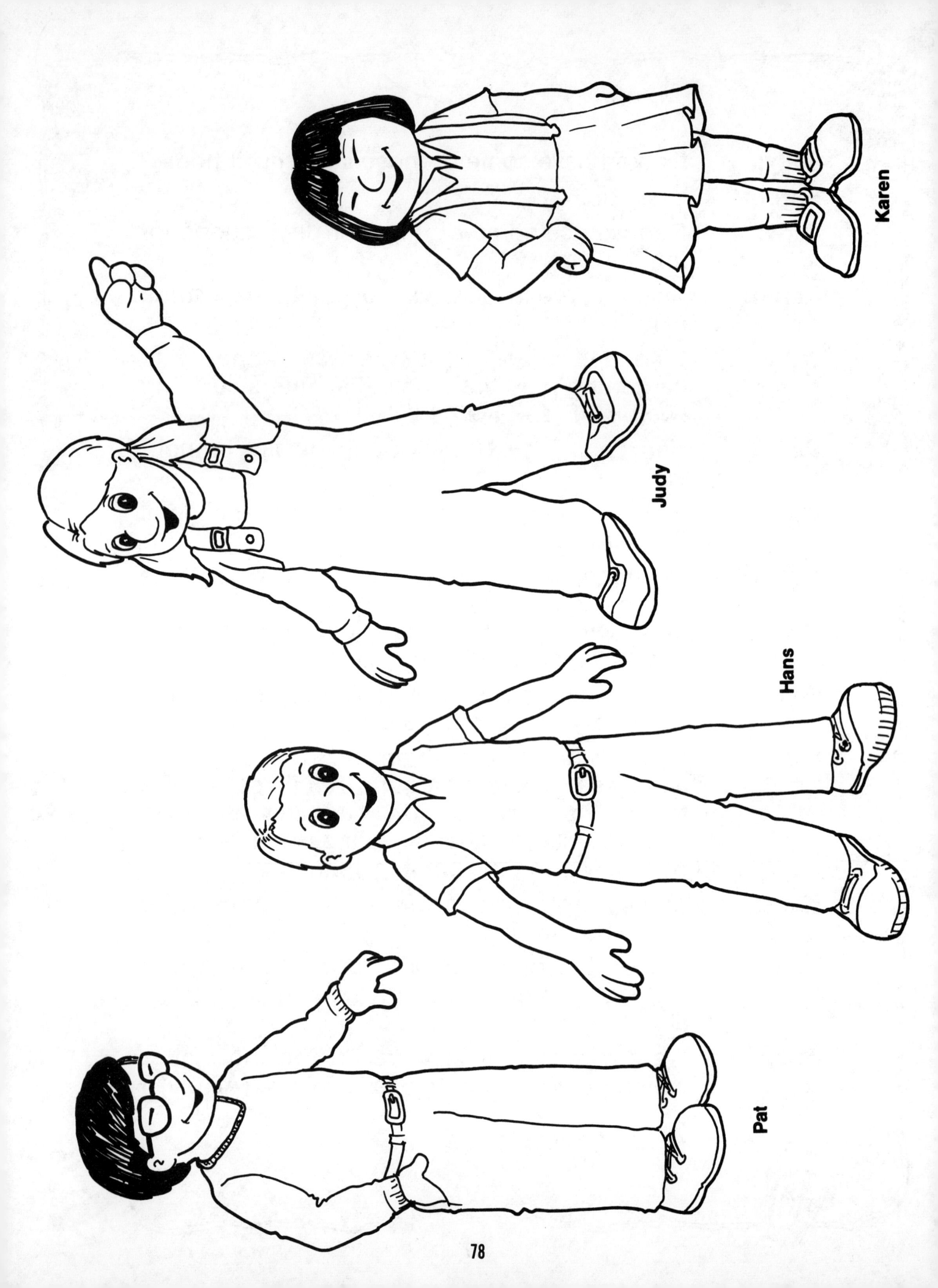

Judy

Hans

Pat

78

a party hat

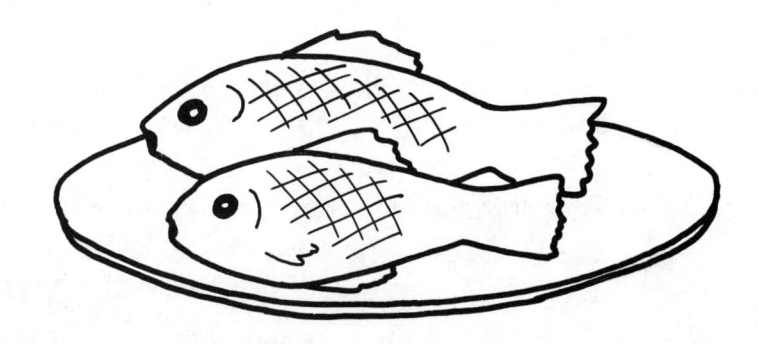

a platter of herring

fish lantern

flower lantern

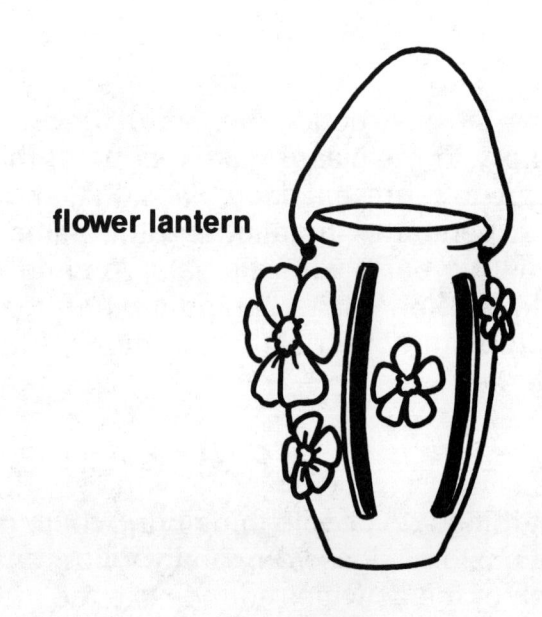

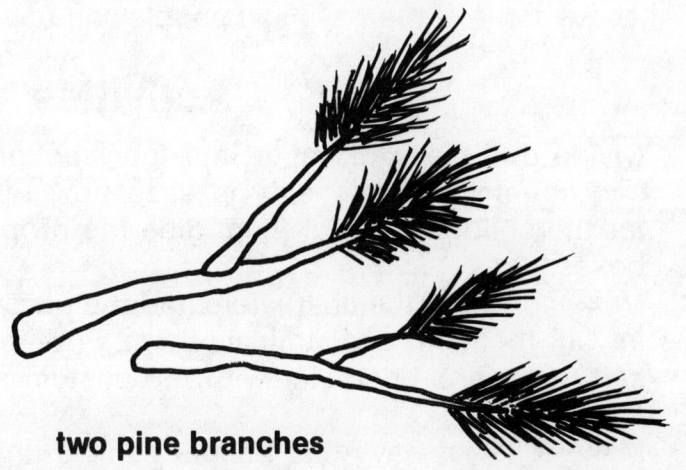

two pine branches

79

For the Teacher

The calendar that we use with our children is the Gregorian calendar and is based on the sun. This is explained further in the holiday story of Leap Year Day.

The Japanese New Year's celebration is called Osho Gatsu. The gong is sounded for the 108 human weaknesses that are mentioned in the Buddhist teachings.

The Chinese New Year's celebration is called Yuan Tan (Wahn Tahn).

Presenting the Story

Preschool and Kindergarten

Read the puppet play to the children using the four puppets and props that are presented. Color them as they should be before you use them. When the play is over, leave the puppets out for the children to see by gluing them onto sticks and sticking the sticks in globs of clay. Place the props near the child to whom they belong.

First Grade and Above

Follow the instructions above or have one of the reading groups present the story to the class. Make a copy of the play for each of the four children who are to represent Judy, Hans, Pat, and Karen. Mark the copy as belonging to that person by highlighting the name of the person in the character list and all his parts with the same highlighter. Use a puppet stage or let the children sit on chairs behind a piano that can be used as the stage. Locate the different countries on the globe and the different New Year's dates on a calendar.

Follow-up Questions

What things do people think bring them good luck?
What customs does your family follow on New Year's?
Which of the activities sounds like the most fun to you?
What are some of the ways that people can be unkind?

Activities

1. Divide one piece of paper into four sections. Write a character's name and country or nationality in each box. Run copies of the story props for the children and let them glue the props onto the paper in the right boxes.
2. Make copies of the characters and the party favors and food. Color them in. Cut them out and laminate them. Put them in a center where children can match the character with the custom and tell the story themselves to each other.
3. Make a list of ways that people can be unkind. Number the ways. Add to them as children think of new ways. Clap hands each day the number of times to remind the children not to be unkind.

Celebration

Have a parade using a dragon and have the children form the dragon as suggested below. Parade through the school.

Return to the room and have a tasting party, wearing party hats.

Dragon

Buy five yards of cheap green cotton fabric to be the dragon's body. Make a dragon's head out of a grocery sack by painting it green with a large red mouth and eyes and gluing on large green ears and yellow eyes. Paint one folded section of newspaper yellow, one red, and one orange. Let it dry thoroughly. Tear into strips and glue on as fire from the mouth.

Tasting Table

Separate bowls of food with small pieces of each of the following foods and any other foods from Germany, Japan, or China.

black-eyed peas	pickled herring
Chinese fortune cookies	rice

Set up a table for the tasting party and have one toothpick or spoon for each child. Let them walk around the table and select one small piece of each of the foods to taste. Provide each of them with a napkin into which the food may be placed if they don't like it.

Hats

Give each child a piece of folded newspaper to color or paint with thin tempera. Let it dry. Roll the paper into a cone shape and form a hat for each child to wear on New Year's Eve. Decorate the hats further with squares of tissue paper, glitter, sticks or more paint.

Story Picture

_____
_____
_____
_____
_____

Chinese New Year

Story Picture

_____
_____
_____
_____
_____

New Year's Eve   New Year's Day
December 31   January 1

Martin Luther King, Jr.
Birthday Celebration

Some holidays are new and some holidays are old. We have celebrated some holidays for only a short period of time. Others we have celebrated for many years. Martin Luther King, Jr., Day is one of the newer holidays. It was first celebrated in 1986.

Martin Luther King, Jr., was a black man who died before most of you were born. He grew up in the South where black people were not treated the same as white people. As a boy M.L., as he was called, began to think about the differences in the way people were treated. He did not like it.

M.L. felt that all people should be treated the same. The color of their skin did not matter. When M.L. grew up he wanted to do something to *convince* people that this was true.

M.L. studied hard to become a minister and a leader of his church. He practiced speaking. Black people came from all over the South to hear what M.L. had to say. They became convinced that what he had to say was true. All people should be treated the same.

Sadly, black people still were not treated the same by their white neighbors. M.L. formed parades for *civil rights*. He and his friends were arrested when they marched in these parades demanding that they be treated equally. No matter how M.L. was treated, he did not hit back. He said that the way to change attitudes was in a peaceful way. He called this belief *nonviolent protest*.

Slowly M.L. and his friends began to convince some white people that all people should be treated the same. But some white people were afraid of this change. One such man shot and killed Martin Luther King, Jr., when he was only 39 years old.

M.L.'s friends wanted to *honor* his memory. They suggested that we celebrate Martin Luther King, Jr., Day each year on his birthday. It took many years for his friends to convince Congress to honor him. Finally, in 1983 Congress gave its OK for the holiday, and later President Ronald Reagan added his approval. Many of M.L.'s friends were with the President when January 15th was named as Martin Luther King, Jr., Day.

This holiday is a time to think about what M.L. had to say and how he wanted people to live. People of all colors should be treated in the same way. Hitting back will not solve problems. Problems can be settled in peaceful ways.

For the Teacher

Martin Luther King, Jr., was born on January 15, 1929, in his grandparents' home in Atlanta, Georgia, where his father was a minister of a local Baptist Church. He died on April 4, 1968, in Memphis, Tennessee, when he stepped out onto his motel balcony to join friends for dinner and was shot.

Dr. King's coffin was taken through the streets of Atlanta on an old farm wagon pulled by two mules as a symbol of his concern for the poor. Over 100,000 people walked behind the wagon. He was buried in Atlanta with the words "Free at last! Free at last! Thank God Almighty, I'm free at last!" printed on his crypt.

Presenting the Story

Preschool, Kindergarten, First Grade and Above

This story is one that needs to be read to young children with compassion and concern for a person who was concerned for others. Their questions should be answered with as much honesty as they can understand.

Follow-up Questions

What types of things did M.L. talk about when he preached?
Why do you think he was concerned that people be nice to each other?
How do you feel when people are not nice to you?

Activities

Role-play some violent and nonviolent ways of solving problems with the children.

I Want That Toy

Put the children into a circle on the floor. Ask one child to volunteer to be a child playing with one of the children's favorite toys, one over which there are frequently arguments.

Give each child in the circle a happy face card or a sad face card. Go around the circle lettering each child in the circle. Tell the child with the toy that *"I want that toy."*

If the child has a happy face card, have him say something that is the nice way to share the toy or get the toy that he wants. Examples: "May I have that when you are finished?" "Could I please play with you?"

If the child has a sad face card, have him say something that is an unacceptable way to get what he wants. Examples: "Gimme that toy right now." "I'll beat you up if you don't give that to me right now."

Right and Not Right

Write these phrases and other similar ones on 3" x 5" index cards. Make two large cards that say *right* and *not right*.

Gimme that toy.
I'll smack you.
That's mine. Give it to me.

I'll tell the teacher on you.

May I have that toy, please?
May we play together?
Will you give me that toy when you are finished?
I'll give you my toy if I can have yours.

Pass the 3" x 5" cards out to some of the children. Have them read their cards. (You might have to read it to them first.) Have the group of children tell the child where to go—to the *right* sign or to the *not right* sign.

Parade for Nonviolence

Have the children make a poster for each of the rules in the room. (Be nice. Keep to your own space. Listen. Follow directions.) To review the rules, let the children parade around the room with their placards to remind each other of the nonviolent ways in the classroom.

Famous Friends

Read the story about the life of Martin Luther King, Jr., in *Pathfinders* from the Famous Friend Series. It tells more about his life as a child and provides discussion questions and activities for young children.

First and Second Grade
Independent Study Cards

Glue each one of these tasks onto a 3" x 5" index card and leave in a center or on a discovery table for children to pursue in their independent learning time.

Write down 3 things that make you angry. Think about ways you can get things peacefully without fighting or arguing. Write your solutions across from your problems.

Choose 3 facts from the story about M.L. and see if you can find those facts in a different book. Write down the facts and the book you found them in.

Make a list of 10 famous people you know about. Read about the people and see if you can find out what race each person is. List the race beside each name. Try to find famous people of various races.

M.L. wanted all people to be treated equally. Can you think of a saying, proverb, or verse that tells us to live peacefully. Write it down and put a border around it.

Story Picture

_____
_____
_____
_____

**Martin Luther King, Jr., Day
January 15**

Abraham Lincoln's Birthday
George Washington's Birthday
A Play

Characters: Martha Custis Washington
Mary Todd Lincoln

Mary: (from off stage) Martha, Martha Custis Washington, where are you going in such a rush?

Martha: (appearing on stage) I'm late for my talk with the girls and boys of _____'s classroom, Mary.
(supply name of your class)

Mary: (appearing on stage) Oh, forgive me for interrupting. (Mary moves back the way she entered.)

Martha: Mary, please stay. I'm here to tell the youngsters about the important birthdays that we celebrate in February. What better person to help me tell the story than you!

Mary: Thank you, Martha. I appreciate the invitation.

Martha: My name is Martha Custis Washington. I am the wife of George Washington, the first President of the United States. This is Mary Todd Lincoln. She is married to Abraham Lincoln, who was the sixteenth President of the United States.

Mary: Although Martha and I did not live at the same time in history, we are here today in "make believe" time to tell you about the celebrations of our husbands' birthdays.

Martha: Both of our husbands, George Washington and Abraham Lincoln, were Presidents during *difficult* times. Both men were great leaders of this country.

Mary: And both men were born in February. My husband, Abraham, was born on February 12th. Martha's husband, George, was born on the 22nd of February.

Martha: Just like us, George and Abraham lived at different times.

Mary: I remember that Abraham talked often of George's contributions to the development of this country.

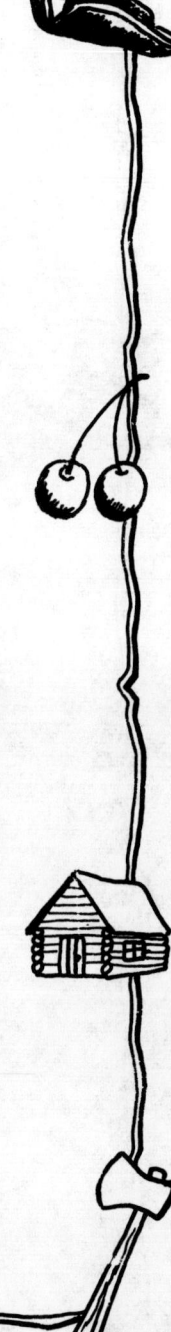

Abraham Lincoln's Birthday
George Washington's Birthday

Martha: Yes, George was really a "homebody." That means that he enjoyed staying home on our plantation, Mount Vernon, in Virginia. But when the United States needed him to lead the country in its battle for independence and to become the very first President of the United States, he felt it was his duty to leave Mount Vernon.

Mary: Have people always celebrated his birthday?

Martha: When George was alive, we gave parties at Mount Vernon. If he was away from home, the military men played fife and drum concerts for him.
After George died in 1799 people remembered his birthday each year in some way. I understand that now there is a President's Day which is celebrated the third Monday in February.

Mary: Yes, that's right, Martha. For many years after Abraham died in 1865, there were two separate holidays. Lincoln's birthday on February 12th and Washington's Birthday on February 22nd. Recently people observe only one holiday with President's Day.

Martha: I'm so proud of our husbands, Mary. It's nice to think that they were so important that they are still remembered today.

Mary: I think of it a different way, Martha. Aren't the youngsters lucky to have two such men to remember and look up to?

Martha: Oh, Mary, that's a nice thought. I'll have to tell George what you said. (She exits stage right.)

Mary: Yes, I must remember to tell Abraham what I did today. (She exits stage left.)

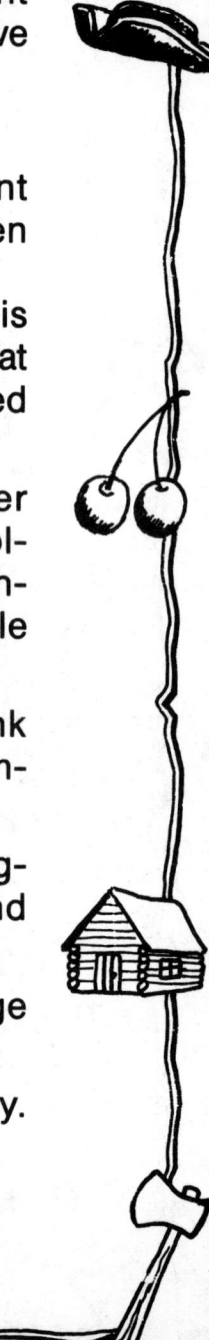

Mary Todd Lincoln

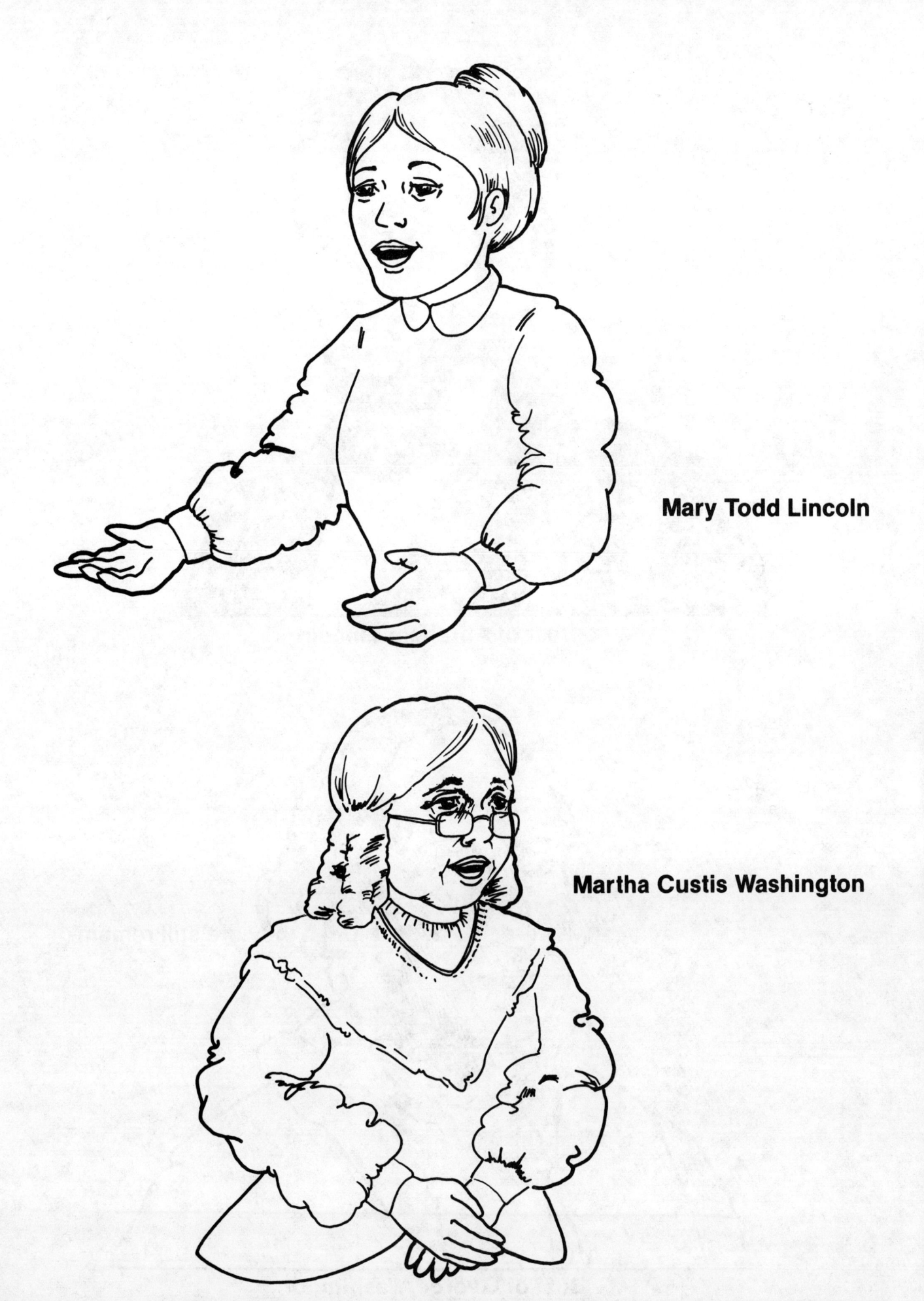

Martha Custis Washington

Bust of Abraham Lincoln

Bust of George Washington

For the Teacher

George Washington was born in 1732 and died in 1799. He married Martha Custis in 1759. She was the same age as he.

Abraham Lincoln was born in 1809 and was assassinated in 1865. He married Mary Todd in 1842. She was nine years younger, born in 1818. In 1892 Illinois began celebrating Lincoln's birthday as a state holiday. Other states followed.

Presenting the Story

Preschool and Kindergarten

Use the face and blouse patterns suggested for Mary and Martha. Color them and affix them to tennis balls. Cover the top and back of each ball with yarn for hair. To make the skirt, fold a piece of material or construction paper (gray for Martha and black for Mary) accordion style and glue to the blouse. Place a dowel into the tennis ball in order to hold the puppet. The two puppets can be made to sit. Make two chairs out of small boxes and cover with material scraps.

First Grade and Above

Follow the instructions above or have the children make the puppets and skirts themselves. They can also make puppets of the men. On a time line find when both were President. Show the children the four-year blocks of time.

Follow-up Questions

Why did Mary think her husband was important?
Why did Martha think her husband was important?
Why do you think your mom is important? Your dad?

Activities

1. Give each child a copy of the pictures of the men and of the women. Cut out the pictures and glue them to the top of a blank sheet of paper. List words that describe each of the people.
2. Put out several coins for the children and let them find Lincoln and Washington on the coins. Have each one draw a picture of the penny and quarter near the portraits of Lincoln and Washington.

Art Activities

1. Make cherry trees for Washington and share the story of George Washington and the cherry tree. Let children paper punch red construction paper to make the cherries and cut out trunks and leaves from construction paper.
2. Make log cabins from Lincoln Logs or brown strips of paper for Lincoln. Read about his life in the Famous Friends Series, *Presidential Leaders*.
3. Make tall Lincoln hats from black paper and adjust band to fit.

Celebration

Wear the Lincoln hats and eat cherry pie.

Story Picture

_____
_____
_____
_____
_____

Abraham Lincoln's Birthday
February 12

Story Picture

_____
_____
_____
_____
_____
_____

**George Washington's Birthday
February 22**

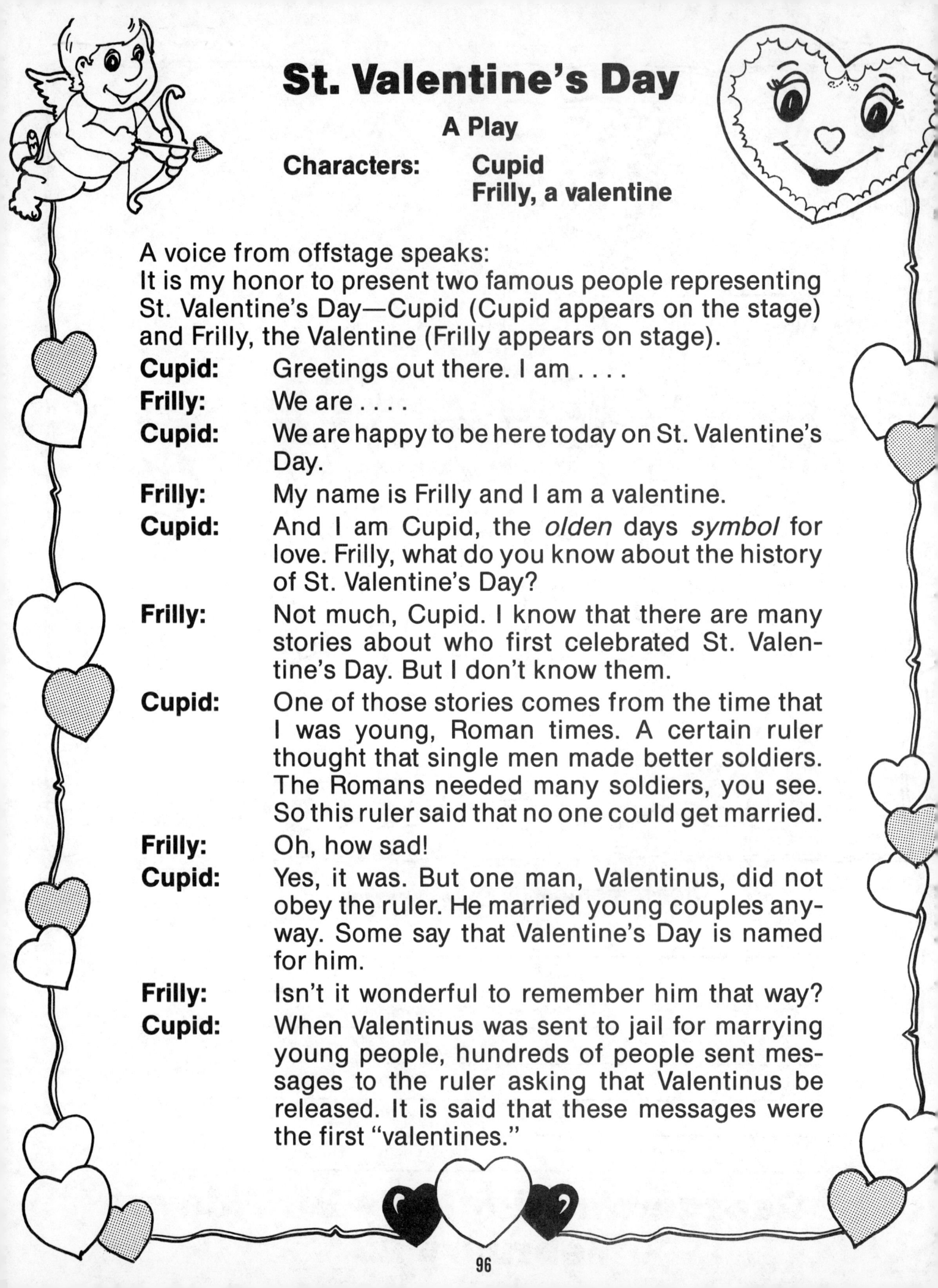

St. Valentine's Day

A Play

Characters: Cupid
Frilly, a valentine

A voice from offstage speaks:
It is my honor to present two famous people representing St. Valentine's Day—Cupid (Cupid appears on the stage) and Frilly, the Valentine (Frilly appears on stage).

Cupid: Greetings out there. I am . . . .
Frilly: We are . . . .
Cupid: We are happy to be here today on St. Valentine's Day.
Frilly: My name is Frilly and I am a valentine.
Cupid: And I am Cupid, the *olden* days *symbol* for love. Frilly, what do you know about the history of St. Valentine's Day?
Frilly: Not much, Cupid. I know that there are many stories about who first celebrated St. Valentine's Day. But I don't know them.
Cupid: One of those stories comes from the time that I was young, Roman times. A certain ruler thought that single men made better soldiers. The Romans needed many soldiers, you see. So this ruler said that no one could get married.
Frilly: Oh, how sad!
Cupid: Yes, it was. But one man, Valentinus, did not obey the ruler. He married young couples anyway. Some say that Valentine's Day is named for him.
Frilly: Isn't it wonderful to remember him that way?
Cupid: When Valentinus was sent to jail for marrying young people, hundreds of people sent messages to the ruler asking that Valentinus be released. It is said that these messages were the first "valentines."

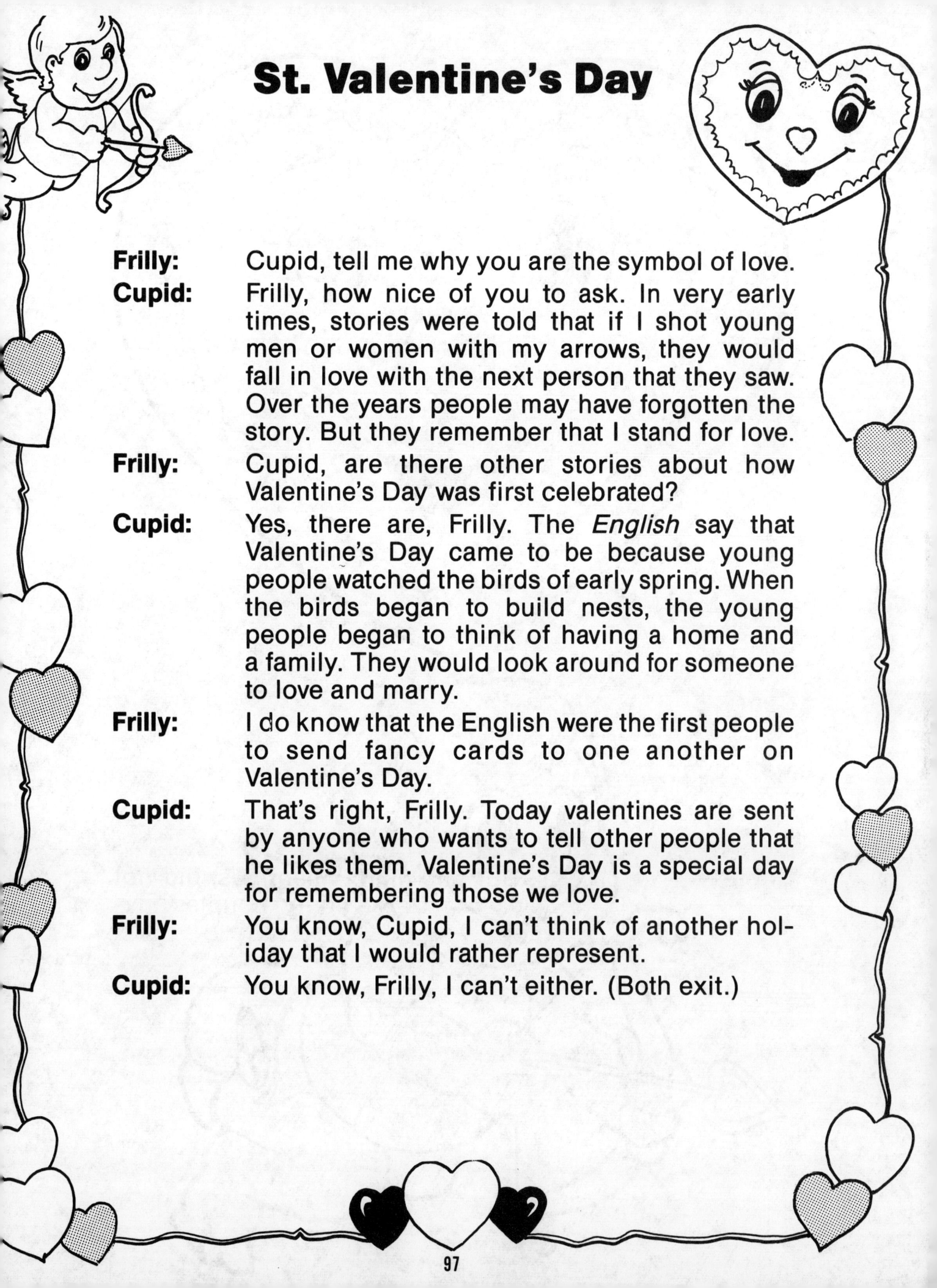

St. Valentine's Day

Frilly: Cupid, tell me why you are the symbol of love.

Cupid: Frilly, how nice of you to ask. In very early times, stories were told that if I shot young men or women with my arrows, they would fall in love with the next person that they saw. Over the years people may have forgotten the story. But they remember that I stand for love.

Frilly: Cupid, are there other stories about how Valentine's Day was first celebrated?

Cupid: Yes, there are, Frilly. The *English* say that Valentine's Day came to be because young people watched the birds of early spring. When the birds began to build nests, the young people began to think of having a home and a family. They would look around for someone to love and marry.

Frilly: I do know that the English were the first people to send fancy cards to one another on Valentine's Day.

Cupid: That's right, Frilly. Today valentines are sent by anyone who wants to tell other people that he likes them. Valentine's Day is a special day for remembering those we love.

Frilly: You know, Cupid, I can't think of another holiday that I would rather represent.

Cupid: You know, Frilly, I can't either. (Both exit.)

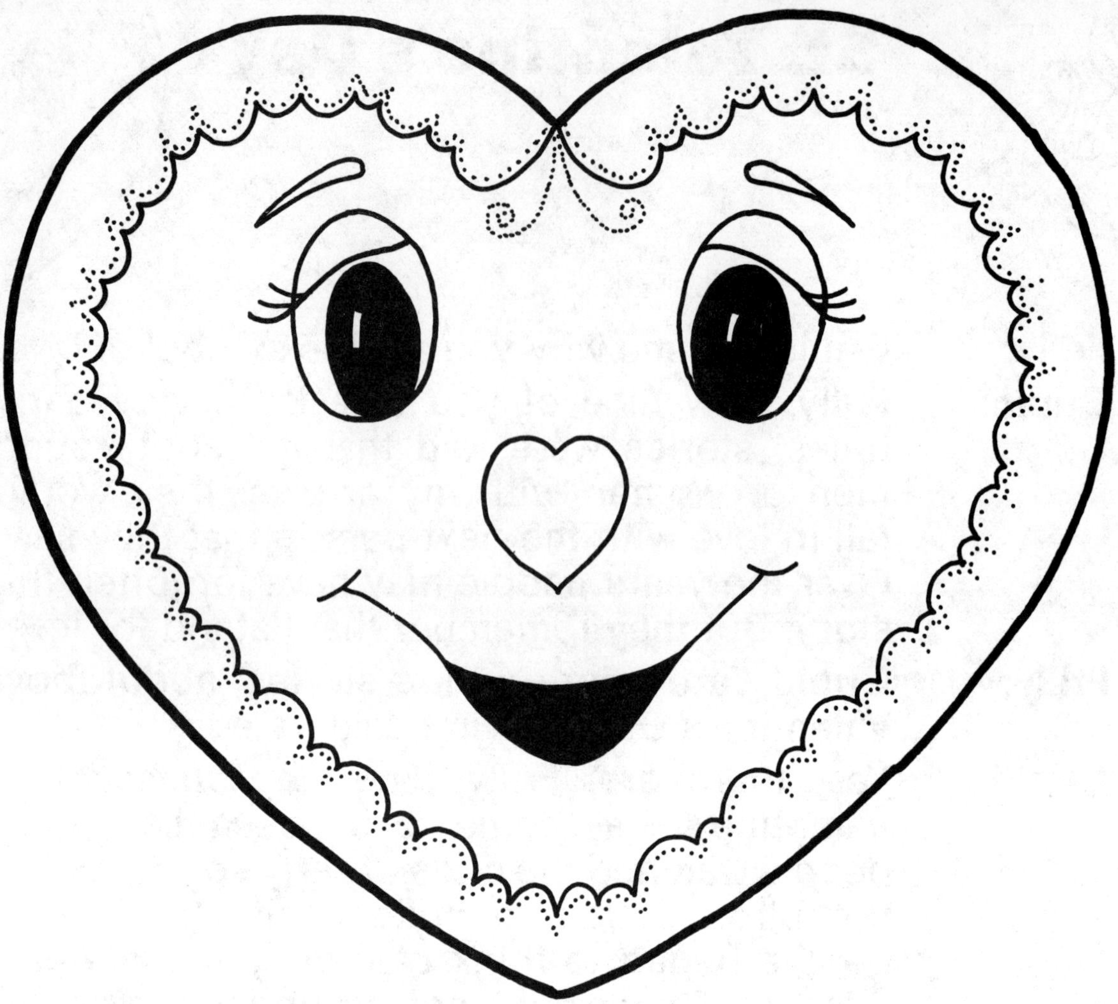

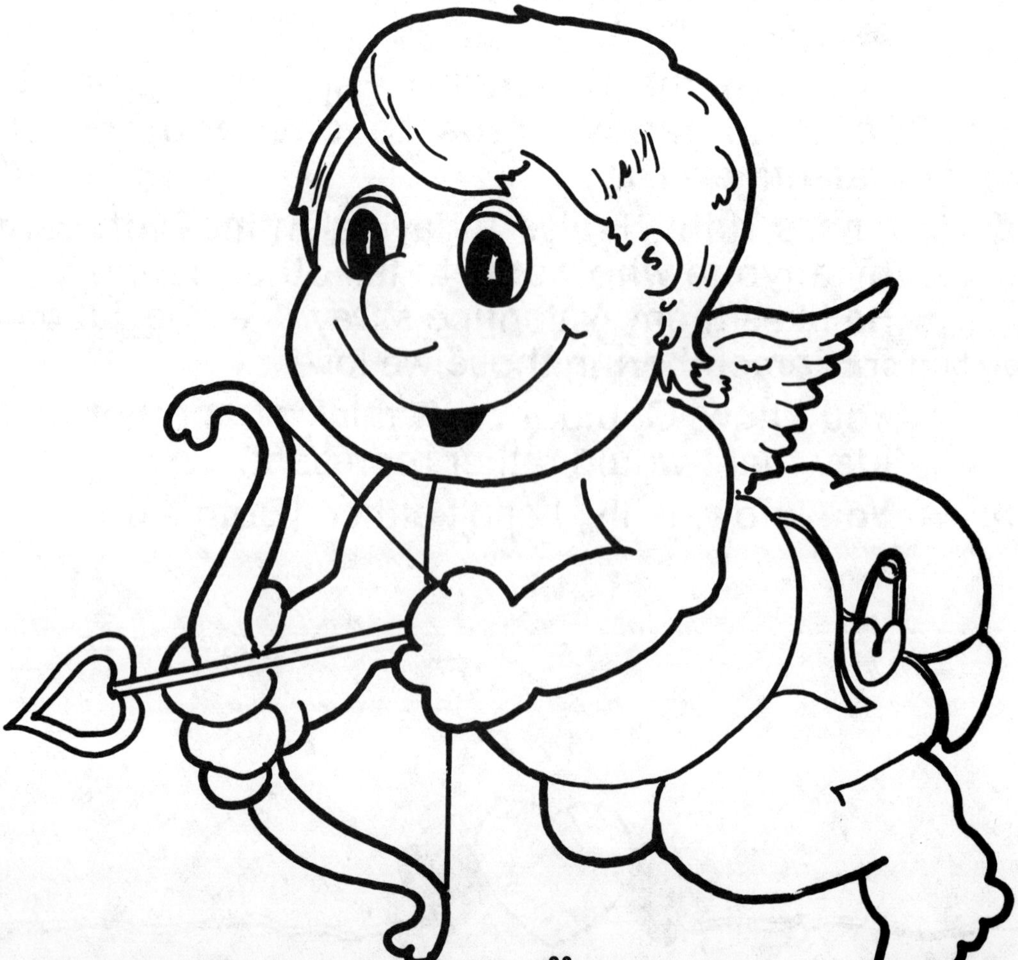

For the Teacher

St. Valentine's Day is one of those days that could easily be exited from our schedules if we called it St. Valentine's Day. It might be that you want to white out the *St.* throughout the story and in all the work you have displayed.

Two versions of how and why St. Valentine's Day came about are presented here. Others are available. You might want to check other resources or remind children that these are but a few of the stories about St. Valentine's Day.

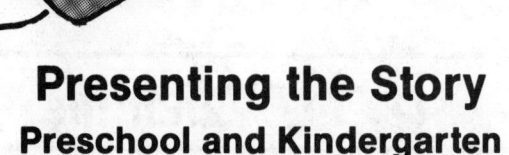

Presenting the Story
Preschool and Kindergarten

The children are always excited about Valentine's Day, even the young ones who know very little about it. Just the thought of getting "mail" excites them.

Color the two puppets. Frill up Frilly with a doily, if you have some available. Present the two puppets and let children learn the names of them before you begin the story. If you have no puppet stage, put the two behind your back after you have introduced them and begin.

First Grade and Above

Let two of your children color the puppets and frill up Frilly. Give the script to two others who are two of the better readers or actors, not to memorize, but to read several times and paraphrase into their own words.

Let the two children present the script to the children with your help as needed.

Follow-up Questions

Why didn't the Roman ruler want the young soldiers to get married?

What happened when Cupid shot you with an arrow? Do you suppose that the arrow hurt or made you happy?

Activities

1. Let children think of words that end with the same sound as the word *Frilly*. If they are sophisticated enough, have them write some two or four-line poems. (Billy, chilly, dilly, hilly, silly, will he?)

2. Write the words *I Love You* on the board for children to learn to write and to use on valentines of their own making. Some of the older ones might like to make the letters into a heart shape or to make the letter *o* the shape of hearts.

3. Place several heart patterns out for the children to trace and cut out. They can then make their own valentines to give to their classmates and friends. Put vocabulary words that they request on a large heart.

Celebration

Present the play to the class. Cut out an arrow for each child. Shoot each child in the room with one of Cupid's arrows and as you give it to him, tell him what a wonderful child he is. Have the children pass out valentines to others in the class by placing signed cards in the children's special boxes. Celebrate with a red brunch.

Arrows

These arrows are not meant for killing but for telling others that you like them. Cut one out for each child in your class and give each a valentine's hug.

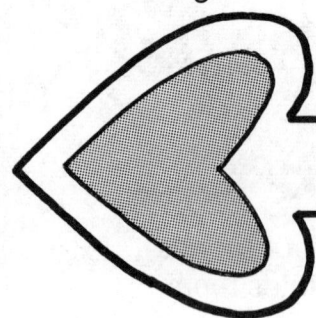

Be My Valentine

Valentines

Let the children make their own valentines. Provide paper: red, white, pink, violet, lime green, rose
glue: white glue, paste, or glue sticks
heart patterns
doilies
yarn
scissors
tape
staplers

Valentine Boxes

Ask parents at the first of the year to save shoe boxes for you. Let the children decorate their mail (shoe) boxes with valentines they make. If they are too young, cut out several hearts of various shapes and buy some stickers or let them take the boxes home for a family project.

Red Brunch (or Lunch)

Peanut butter and strawberry jelly sandwiches, using bread made with red food coloring.
Apples
Red sugar cookies with pink icing in heart shapes

Tasting Tray

Beets	Strawberries	Raspberries
Red Bell Peppers	Fun Fruits	Red Hots
Cherries	Red Fruit Loops	Cherry Life Savers

Story Picture

Valentine's Day   February 14

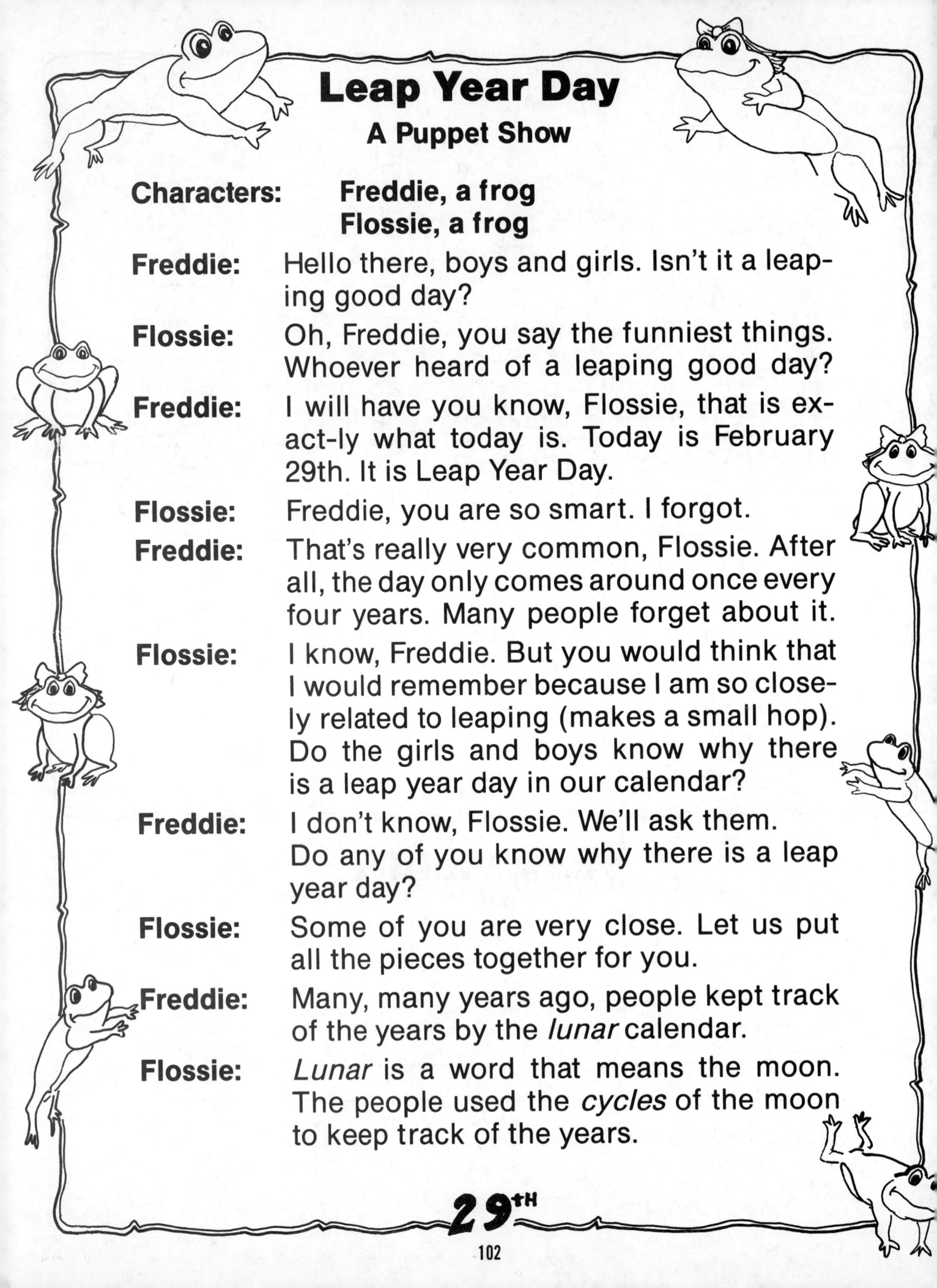

Leap Year Day
A Puppet Show

Characters: Freddie, a frog
Flossie, a frog

Freddie: Hello there, boys and girls. Isn't it a leaping good day?

Flossie: Oh, Freddie, you say the funniest things. Whoever heard of a leaping good day?

Freddie: I will have you know, Flossie, that is ex-act-ly what today is. Today is February 29th. It is Leap Year Day.

Flossie: Freddie, you are so smart. I forgot.

Freddie: That's really very common, Flossie. After all, the day only comes around once every four years. Many people forget about it.

Flossie: I know, Freddie. But you would think that I would remember because I am so close-ly related to leaping (makes a small hop). Do the girls and boys know why there is a leap year day in our calendar?

Freddie: I don't know, Flossie. We'll ask them.
Do any of you know why there is a leap year day?

Flossie: Some of you are very close. Let us put all the pieces together for you.

Freddie: Many, many years ago, people kept track of the years by the *lunar* calendar.

Flossie: *Lunar* is a word that means the moon. The people used the *cycles* of the moon to keep track of the years.

29ᵀᴴ

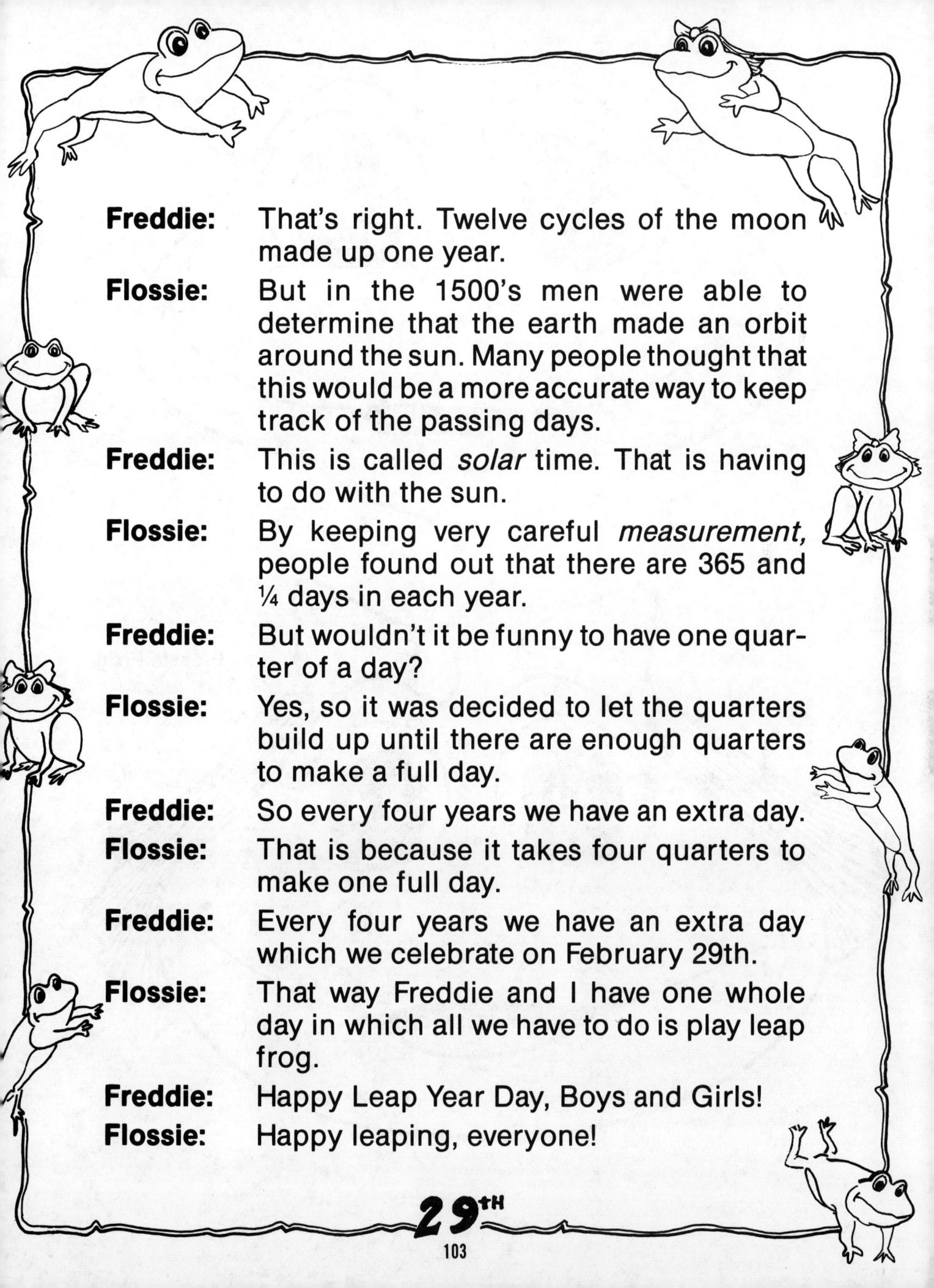

Freddie: That's right. Twelve cycles of the moon made up one year.

Flossie: But in the 1500's men were able to determine that the earth made an orbit around the sun. Many people thought that this would be a more accurate way to keep track of the passing days.

Freddie: This is called *solar* time. That is having to do with the sun.

Flossie: By keeping very careful *measurement*, people found out that there are 365 and ¼ days in each year.

Freddie: But wouldn't it be funny to have one quarter of a day?

Flossie: Yes, so it was decided to let the quarters build up until there are enough quarters to make a full day.

Freddie: So every four years we have an extra day.

Flossie: That is because it takes four quarters to make one full day.

Freddie: Every four years we have an extra day which we celebrate on February 29th.

Flossie: That way Freddie and I have one whole day in which all we have to do is play leap frog.

Freddie: Happy Leap Year Day, Boys and Girls!

Flossie: Happy leaping, everyone!

Freddy Frog

Flossie Frog

Story Picture

_____
_____
_____
_____
_____

Leap Year Day   **February 29**

Resources

General

Burnett	*The First Book of Holidays*
Flemming and Hamilton	*Resources for Creative Teaching in Early Childhood Education*
Grigoli	*Patriotic Holidays and Celebrations*
Harkness	*Legends of the Holidays*
Hazeltine	*Anniversaries and Holidays*
Van Straalen	*The Book of Holidays Around the World*
Schauffler	*The Days We Celebrate* (2 volumes)
Sesame Street Magazine	December, 1985

Specific Holidays

Hanukkah
- Drucker — *Hanukkah: Eight Days, Eight Lights*

Columbus Day
- Carroll and Wells — *Founders*, Famous Friends Series, Good Apple, Inc.

Christmas
- Holz — *The Christmas Spider*

New Year's
- Young — *The Rooster's Horns*

Martin Luther King Day
- Wells and Carroll — *Pathfinders*, Famous Friends Series, Good Apple, Inc.
- Bone-Jones — Martin Luther King, Jr.

President's Day
- Aten — *Presidential Leaders*, Famous Friends Series, Good Apple, Inc.
- Smith — *George Washington* (Great American Series)
- Smith — *Abraham Lincoln* (Great American Series)